G000097762

women
OF
INFLUENCE

Shaping the world through
focused impact, business improvement
and positive change

PRESENTED BY
HAYLEY PAIGE INTERNATIONAL

Elly Charles | Elizabeth Davis | Rochelle Gilburn
Layla Hinchen | Zina Kular | Caroline Leckey
Charlie Mac | Emma Matthews | Nelly Storm
Cheryl Thompson | Arianna Trapani

NOTEBOOK
PUBLISHING

First published in 2021 by Notebook Publishing of
Notebook Group Limited, 20–22 Wenlock Road,
London, N1 7GU.

www.notebookpublishing.com

ISBN: 9781913206604

A CIP catalogue record for this book is available
from the British Library.

Typeset by Notebook Publishing.

For the Women of Influence of the world, who continue to push forward with the goal of impact, business improvement and positive change.

Without you, the world would be a lesser place.

ELLY CHARLES

*International Psychic Medium & Spiritual Training
Provider, guiding women along their spiritual journey
to take charge of their empowered choices and move
forward along the path of their true soul purpose*

TRUST IN THE PATH THAT was laid out for
you: your soul already knows it.

My eyes opened as I lay there on the
floor, having had yet another seizure, completely
unexplained and out of the blue. What was going
on? Why, why, *why* had this happened *again*? Who
or what was trying to stop me in my tracks?

Oh, man. I had never had my body *not*
physically function correctly for me. I felt scared,
alone, and in a lot of pain. Sometimes, when you are

in so much pain, it is hard to *not* focus on the negatives—and oh my gosh, the negatives were flying in. However, being the spiritual person I am, I had to find a way to pull myself out of this. *Elly, remember the light; the light that you have channelled for so many years; the light that you have connected to for so long. You saw the light during your seizures, and you saw your spirit guides there with you* is what I would say to myself. *Elly, they are not going to kill you off yet; only when you have achieved all that they have led you to do* is another thing I would say to myself. Sometimes, you've just gotta have a pep talk with yourself.

Elly, you will not die when there is still so much for you to do.

Elly, remember your truth.

These are the words I would find myself thinking over and over when I was dealing with the head pain from my seizures, having come so far along my journey and having had such a transformation in life already. Who or what was trying to stop me in my tracks? Being the spiritual being that I am, I have grown to be very accepting of what comes my way, and being the psychic that I am, I have also learnt to understand the signs of when something is going to happen that might shake up my life—and I have learnt to trust every single motion in life. This is because I now understand that everything happens for a reason, and that if we can trust in the signs, guidance, thoughts, and feelings that we are receiving on a daily basis, then we will become much more equipped to deal with anything that comes our way.

You see, some would say that I have done very well for myself—which I would respond with yes, I have; however, you can't tempt fate: if something is meant to happen to shake things up, then it will happen. It's about how you process it and heal from it that counts.

So, I found myself going through the motions of healing myself and doing the very thing I knew best when it came to recovering from the seizures that I had experienced: trusting that my spirit guides had my back and that my life was on-track, even if I felt set back. There was something even better for me coming my way. I chose not to see this as a failure or as something to hold me back; I chose to see this as an opportunity to listen to my heart and make some changes that felt right for me and the next stage of my life. You see, I saw this as a sign that my spirit guides were telling that I needed to step into a new direction fully. After learning and developing such a strong powerful spiritual skillset over the years, I now needed to use my skillset to better myself even more to then be able to help even more people.

Through my many years of spiritually guiding so many different women, there was always one question that often came up for them: how do I just trust in my path? How do I trust in my intuition?

How many of you have found yourself asking this same question over and over, especially when you feel so strongly to your very core that you *must* follow a particular route in life, despite all the practical aspects pointing to a totally different path? What's more, how many of you have chosen the path you are were drawn to over the one you thought or everyone else thought was right for you?

It has been so amazing guiding so many inspiring, amazing women along their spiritual journey into really stepping up to take charge of their empowered choices; to moving forward along the path of their true soul purpose.

Over the years, so many women have been waking up feeling, sensing, and just knowing deep within that their calling is upon them, and it's been a true pleasure to hold space for these fabulous women to rise up into their true selves!

You see, I had a very similar experience. At the age of four years old, I was seeing and speaking with spirits; however, as I grew into a young woman, I became very drained and also scared at times of the energy I felt, so much so that I would avoid or even try to block doing spiritual things.

You could say that my younger years started out pretty rough, having suffered with sexual abuse throughout my childhood. As a result, I led a pretty destructive life in my early twenties. This lifestyle, I knew, was due to the pain I was feeling deep in my heart from my previous pain as a child, and unfortunately, the lifestyle I chose was a very intoxicated one. I lived in full-on self-destruct mode.

It wasn't until I was about twenty-five years old that I started to realise the destruction of my ways, and I found myself in a three-year period of detoxing my mind, body, and soul. I completely changed my attitude, my living situation, and the people I associated with; I stopped taking things that were not good for my body and I began to heal and learn so much about myself.

It was only years on, when my spiritual business was fully fledged, that I truly realised just why I had had to go through so much pain and destruction. You see, if I hadn't found my way spiritually, I wouldn't have transformed, and I wouldn't have been able to see my true path and begin to *trust*.

It is hard to understand exactly how we come to trust our intuition, but through coaching my clients,

I often see that truth means many different things for people. The reason why there are so many blocks around our truth is the things that have happened in our past.

Truth in our hearts, to me, feels like a strong *knowing* that you have to go somewhere or do something, even if you have no idea why, or where it will lead to; you just *know* that there is something great that is going to happen. The truth in your heart feels warm and fuzzy, and is an intense, unwavering power that guides you firmly but beautifully to a destination that you are meant to get to. Notably, it can also feel very confusing and scary through the process; the trick is to not bail at the first hurdle.

You see, when you are doing something that feels right and something that you truly enjoy, you will become successful in so many ways: our truth is our given right which our soul already knows; it is our job to discover what is calling our soul and what feels good for us.

That is where I come in: I help you to connect to your deeper calling through my psychic energy by guiding you to really get what your soul has to do next, holding space and teaching you the techniques needed for you to connect in a way in that is so deep that not only are you phasing out things that no longer serve, you but you are also learning how to receive psychic messages for yourself so you can begin to trust.

You see, I believe our contract in life is already laid out for us: we are all energy, and energy is everything—so your soul is energy—just a different density of energy compared to your physical body—and your soul has to work its way through your physical body and this physical realm in the best way it can. This will involve learning, growing, evolving, and collecting the right type of knowledge for yourself to move through the motions of your physical life.

Did you ever wonder how psychics can predict your future?

It is because your future is already written; that contract of life mentioned above was already agreed upon by you. Thus, I ask you to stop and think about those things you want; the dreams and goals you are working on. Why do you think you are seeing them in your mind or thinking of them? The answer is simple: *because they're already yours*. This is why psychics predict things and then they come true: because it's already been agreed.

If this works positively, it also works negatively. I initially found this hard to believe, especially when I was in the height of the horrendous pain I felt in life. I used to ask why I would agree to a contract that was so hard; why I would agree to being unhappy for so long; why on earth I would agree to be abused at an early age. This I just could not get my head around, and especially when I picked up the book *The Secret* by Rhonda Byrne, I found myself feeling actually rather angry about it. The book definitely triggered something in me, and I resisted the thought of a contract. Yet over the years, as I began to let my truth unfold, I found that I became stronger and clearer about why I had been through such heartache. Those psychics' future predictions started to come true. At that time, little did I know that I would become a psychic myself—and not only that, but a psychic who would have clients globally and achieve great success. Yet knowing now what I have been through, seeing my transformation, and feeling the energy of my transformation, it has helped me to gain the energy that I needed to do my life's work, which was written in my life contract.

You, too have a contract.

I ask you to think about this for a moment: where do you find yourself along your life contract? Are you in a bad place at the moment? If so, how are you dealing with it? Are you finding it hard, or are you taking this on? Are you trusting that this will shift? Or if you have been through a hard time along your contract and are now in a much better place, I ask you to look at it and ask yourself whether you understand why that happened. Do you see how you have changed?

Another question for you when thinking of your contract: what do you find yourself wanting, thinking of, or dreaming of often? Are you already receiving what you want? Or do you feel it getting closer?

When we ask ourselves these questions and navigate our thought processes in this way, we are getting to know our hearts and souls in more depth; we are allowing our true purpose to start shining.

When I finally started to surrender to my spiritual side, I decided to set up a little business. I was a single mum at the time, absolutely broke and hurting over the split of me and my daughter's daddy. I felt so lost. By this point, I had already been on a big transformation, having changed the destruction of my ways, and I really hadn't expected a split with my partner—so you can imagine that I sat there, I was tempted to go back to my old ways of partying hard. However, I had already been very much so focusing on myself as a light being, and had started to draw spirituality to me more often, for it was focusing on the light in my heart that got me through my troubled days to start with.

I had been doing readings for people on the side just for practice, so I decided to start charging.

One day, I came back from my spiritual class, and I felt strongly in my heart that I needed to put a post on Facebook offering a reading to anyone who would like one for £15. Back then, I had no business sense at all; I enjoyed it, but I did not financially do well from it at all, and it just wasn't calling to my heart. For me, this wasn't about money; it was just such a strong sensation of it initially felt right to put out there to the world.

I had not one person interested but about five people, so I booked them all in for evenings when my daughter was tucked up in bed, and I began to do these readings. I sat there for hours with these people, some of them even bringing a friend along to listen. I even ended up picking up stuff for the friends. Now looking back, I realise that £15 for three hours of work for two people was less then minimum wage, but I didn't care: it felt good! This energy was buzzing with goodness, and I realised after a while that it felt so great because it was my truth. Not only was I healing though doing this work, but I was also helping others, and I could see that. So now, when I sit and coach women regarding their true purpose or provide them with psychic guidance to connect to their soul contract, I know how immensely important this is because of what was to happen for me after those first initial readings I gave.

Those people went away and without me knowing, each of them chatted to a friend, family member, or work colleague about their readings, and over the weeks, I had more and more people starting to contact me to book in. It naturally flowed like that, and it all felt very easy and exciting as well as uplifting. Within seven months, I had over one hundred five-star reviews, and I had created a wonderful full-time career. I was receiving money, and I was so grateful for that, but also for the lovely things that people were saying about my readings.

Now, I run a successful spiritual business with a global following, not only reading for thousands of people but also coaching and teaching many, including celebrities. Not only that, but I am making the most money I have ever made—and as a result, I was able to invest in my business and create things that I was drawn to. I have been nominated for awards, and actually won an award for Best Spiritual Training Provider, and became highly commended by *The Soul & Spirit* Magazine. Organisations like the famous London College of Psychics speak of my training programmes publicly.

I suddenly realised one day after writing my book that people actually *wanted* to hear what I had to say. That may sound silly, but because I was so in-flow with trusting my heart, I hadn't really thought about the outcome as such; I just knew I had to do the things I wanted to do. My book *Ignite Your Light & Awaken Your Soul* was one of those truths that I had to follow, and on Publication Day, it became an international bestseller in seventeen categories within the spiritual sector, and is to this day still in the top ten bestselling spiritual books. I am now a bestselling author four times over because I trusted the pull of my heart.

When you are so stuck in a rut about the way your life is or how you feel about yourself and the stories you have about yourself, you believe these things you feel, despite them making you feel like rubbish. So, I ask you: is that really your truth?

On the contrary, that is something designed to keep you small and hold you back. Your truth is there, right in your heart.

I ask my clients, 'Where do you think your soul is?' Now, I am asking you, too. Where do you think your soul is? Some say they don't know; some might say their soul is everywhere; some say it's in their heart.

You see, I see my heart as my soul, because where I feel my truth is in my heart. Your heart leads the way, and it is when you listen to the truth in your heart that you will achieve and receive everything that you deserve.

That's why you get the old saying of 'follow your heart, not your head'. Of course, in a more practical sense, some feel they should follow their head rather than their heart—they may think they are being safer that way—, but if you feel unhappy or deflated about following what you feel is practical, then this is a clear indication that you are actually not trusting in your path.

When you listen to the sensations and feelings deep in your heart and take inspired action, your heart will connect to your head to then draw in the things you need to do—not the other way around.

So, on that day years ago, when I decided to put out there to the world that I would like to do a reading for £15, I was listening to the truth in my heart. In that moment, it was an inspired action without me realising the absolute massive significance it was going to have over the next four years of my life and just how far I would come and continue to go. Now, looking back, I see why I did that; I see the bigger picture. Over the last four years of really understanding the way truth feels in my heart and helping thousands of other women understand how it feels for them and bring forth huge transformations and significant spiritual upgrades for them and myself, I truly understand just why knowing your truth is so magnificent—and to me, it is the number one form of energy to move us forward in tremendous ways that will be change your life forever.

So, ladies: I invite you to ask yourself what it is that your soul is telling you to do. Do you feel your spirit guides gathering, ready to call in your true desires? Are you ready to take the next step into really understanding the depth of trust and your truth? If so, I invite you to get in touch with me. You can connect with me on my social media, either on Facebook or Instagram. I offer private one-to-one coaching as well as readings—or if it's group connection you are looking for, I have courses and workshops online and in person. I also run my School of Spirituality membership. Alternatively, you can immerse yourself in one of my beautiful retreats.

As I always say, if you are dedicated to up-levelling your spirituality, then I am dedicated to guiding you.

Let's see where it takes you. I am so excited to share this space with you and to see your path light up. Your soul knows what to do, so it's time to listen!

Contact Elly

Should my story have resonated with you, you can connect with me via the following platforms. I look forward to hearing from you! You can also purchase my book Ignite Your Light & Awaken Your Soul at https://elly.convertri.com/ and access my media kit for podcasts, TV, and radio bookings at https://lnkw.co/ellycharlesmediakit.

 www.ellycharlesmediumship.com

 www.facebook.com/ellycharlesmediumship

 @elly_charles_psychicmedium

ELIZABETH DAVIS

Leadership Coach & Trainer elevating females for success in leadership roles

WOMEN ARE STRONG, POWERFUL, NATURAL-BORN leaders. I have always believed it.

Growing up, I was told that I could do anything I wanted to do, be anything I wanted to be, and that being a girl was *not* a disadvantage. I didn't question this, and I didn't let my gender stop me from making choices like doing woodwork instead of textiles at school, despite being the only girl in that class, or applying for the job that I wanted, even though at that time it had an all-male team.

I will admit I took equality for granted: I had options; I could vote; I could drive; I could access education; I could choose any profession I wanted. As a young girl, I thought the fight had been won: many courageous women before me had fought for our rights, and I had been lucky enough to be born in a time and place where I had choices.

Growing up with these choices, I didn't face any obvious signs that equality *hadn't* already been achieved—but it hadn't: it's still a work in progress; sociologist Arlie Russel Hochschild (1989) calls it 'the stalled revolution'. The more experience I have and the more learning I do, the more I realise that equality is still a long way off.

Unfortunately, the mission to tackle the ingrained issue of gender bias will be ongoing for many years to come. As an example of ongoing bias, many still hold the opinion that women can't drive cars or park as well as men. Having previously been a driving instructor, I have had many fantastic female students who could not only drive better than my male students but were no harder to teach to park. I didn't personally find gender to factor into how I taught my students: each individual learned differently, and the outcome had nothing to do with gender. This stereotype will probably not change any time soon—especially not when all bad parking videos on YouTube are of women doing twenty-point manoeuvres.

Society has a presence that is hard to ignore: business marketing and the media are wired towards biases that unconsciously reinforce them in society. When girls show leadership skills at a young age, they are bossy; when boys do, they are enthusiastic. Girls still face pressure to look out for marriage from a young age and are often encouraged to prioritise marriage and family over career. Even I was told to find a rich man and I wouldn't have to worry! Professional ambition is encouraged in men, but optional for women. Being ambitious is still seen as a negative trait for women, and often comes with a social penalty. In an interview, TV presenter Clare Balding said she had been referred to as being 'very ambitious' as if this was a negative thing because she was a woman. I completely agree with her response when she says, 'Too bloody right I'm ambitious! Why shouldn't I be? Should I want to come second?'

However, through experiences and social conditioning, women are encouraged to expect less, not take up too much space, and not demand more; we often expect to come second, and this means that women end up feeling less deserving than men—and when women feel less deserving, it creates an entitlement gap that directly impacts the careers of women. This is a persistent problem, where historical societal expectations, family load, and murky corporate systems make it harder for women to rise to the top.

I still believe that every woman is powerful, but I also now believe that most women struggle to believe it—and I was one of them. We hold ourselves back because along the way, we have picked up limiting beliefs from comments made or barriers felt, and because we have created a box for ourselves accordingly.

The choices were all available for me, but as I got older, I lost my confidence in myself and in my ability to perform well in my choices. Many tiny, seemingly insignificant moments can add up, and stereotypes creep in until it is hard to push away the self-doubt. I was told that I was too loud and should stay quiet; that I was too much and should learn to play on my own; that I couldn't do things as well as boys could; that I needed to be a 'good girl' to be liked. I was smart, but the assumption was that I would want to be a nurse, not a doctor.

I have never consciously let being a girl be the reason behind my stopping doing something or choosing another option, and I have never stopped believing in the innate power that every woman possesses. However, without realising it, I did stop believing that I had that power.

I was supposed to be a boy: my mum and dad expected me to be a boy and I was going to be a Christopher, right until that moment when I popped out and said hello to the world and became an Elizabeth. I always found this story amusing; it never made me feel unwanted. I knew my parents loved me and were proud of me. However, there were moments when I wondered if they had been disappointed. They tried twice more and ended up having two more daughters. This knowledge may have been the reason behind why I was so determined to do well: to make them proud of me. There was never any pressure from anyone except myself: I wanted to do well at everything, and from a young age, I developed an internal competitive streak. Anytime there was an opportunity to prove girls could do anything boys could do, I was there! I wanted to show that being a girl didn't stop me and that I could do it just as well, if not better.

When puberty came calling and my female friends started bringing in notes to school to skip sports or swimming, I refused to be stopped: I didn't want to put my life on hold once every month, so I figured out what I had to do to continue with my activities as if every day was the same. The knowledge that my own body might work against me once a month did not make me happy.

My passion for women being unstoppable and achieving started there: I refused to be stopped or seen as weak; I looked up to strong women who exuded fearless confidence, and I wanted to grow up to be like them. My mum was someone I looked up to: as a child, she always had the answers I needed, and was always strong, in control, and fearless. I was shocked when I found out she was terrified of lightning because growing up, I had never once seen that fear in her, she did such a good job hiding it. My mum always seemed unstoppable, and I was determined to be the same. Hence, when a boy in my swim class said I couldn't beat him, I did; when my math teacher told me I wouldn't get higher than a D in my exams, I proved him wrong and achieved an A*, the highest grade possible; and when I was told that I wouldn't be able to reverse park a car because I was a girl, I made sure to be the best driver I could be, including some awesome parking skills.

I loved TV shows and movies with strong female characters, such as Terri Hatcher's Lois Lane or Demi Moore in *GI Jane*. *Mulan* has always been my favourite Disney movie because she didn't need a man to find her power; she found it within herself. One of my idols growing up was Tina Turner, especially after I saw the *What's Love Got to Do With It* film: she exudes such strength and passion in her music and onstage despite everything she went through in her personal life. She found her power within and achieved phenomenal success.

Knowing I had a passion for women finding their power and achieving their success was one thing, but knowing what to do with that was another: I was just one girl, and it felt overwhelming at times. I didn't know how I could have any impact in helping other women. I didn't feel that confidence most of the time, and I didn't feel like I had anything valuable to contribute.

By the time I started my first career, I realised that although women had more opportunities available, there still weren't many women at the top of their fields. I was now old enough to vote, but there were no women to vote for, and most of my early managers were men. That's not to say that those early managers weren't decent managers, but that the equality wasn't as evident as I expected.

My first career was in the sport and leisure industry, and it was an accident: I finished university and took a job lifeguarding at a city pool facility. This 'stop-gap' job turned into ten years of working my way through and up into facility management. There were some great female leaders that I worked with, and I learned a lot from them. More often than not, I found their management style to be much more effective and their methods more transparent for the team to understand not just when there were changes, but how those changes had come about. I had some great male managers, but the women I worked with brought a different style and approach that I felt had a better impact.

Unfortunately, during my time in that management position, my dad passed away. It was completely unexpected, and it hit me hard. My stress levels within my job were already fairly significant, but this grief compounded that feeling, and I reached a burnout level I was unable to resolve—and so I left my sport and leisure career behind. In the years following, I lost all confidence in myself: I stopped trusting myself and felt like I made some poor choices, especially in terms of work options.

It took me a long time to regain my sense of self and to start trusting myself again—and in doing so, I also reignited my passion for helping women achieve their success. Not only did I reconnect with this passion, but I finally found a way that I could have an impact. I am no longer just one little girl wishing for a world with more representation of strong women at the top: now, I am a good woman striving to be a better woman while helping the next woman to win.

As I said before, I believe women are natural-born leaders. Unfortunately, not enough women make it to the top: statistically, women are outperforming men when it comes to college qualifications, and they are entering the workforce at a relatively equal rate as their male counterparts; however, by the time they reach middle management, women's representation has dropped to thirty-eight per cent, and it continues to drop the further up we look. Currently, only seven per cent of CEOs at FTSE 100 Companies are women.

The statistics don't fare much better in political leadership: out of one hundred and ninety-three nations, only twenty-two currently have women appointed as the head of state. The global average for female parliamentary participation was only 24.6% in 2019, and according to the Women's Power Index, where a score of one hundred equates to equality for men to women ratio-wise, the highest-scoring country is still only at seventy-four and only twenty-one countries have a score higher than fifty.

For a girl who grew up thinking equality had been won, these statistics shock me. Why are women not making it to the top?

There are many reasons, one obvious one not to be negated being choice: it's a tough road to the top, and many women choose not to push that far. But one reason I want to focus on is the internal barriers we create and carry—the 'glass ceiling' we imagine; the distrust we have in ourselves. Do you believe that you are good enough? Do you trust your instincts to guide you in being a great leader? Are you lead by your fears or your fierce?

A more equal world will not happen overnight, but it *can* happen: person by person, we can create it. I believe female leaders are the key to the solution: conditions for all women will improve when there are more women included in the discussion; more women in leadership roles having their voices heard; more women in power able to challenge established conventions and policy agendas.

Studies in diversity tell us that if we tap into all human resources and talent, our collective performance will improve.

Never has there been more of an opportunity than right now to level the playing field for women in leadership; never before have our workplaces been so disrupted than during COVID-19. This gives us the chance to build back better, making sure no woman is left behind. Before COVID-19, working from home was relatively rare, with only five per cent of employees working from home regularly. However, the pandemic has skipped the processes of change and adjustment and *forced* the change. This has had some advantages in terms of household duties being recognised and shared, and in many cases has created more opportunity for a shared approach to the care of children. A more equal household and a more flexible working environment could provide more opportunity and potential for women to progress more.

The pandemic, while devastating in many ways, has also provided an interesting opportunity to see the impact female leaders have while navigating a crisis. Even with so few female Heads of State, this has provided one of the first real opportunities to compare their approach—and therefore, more evidence is now available supporting the positive impact that female leaders have. An article in *The Independent* states, 'Researchers concluded that of one hundred and ninety-three countries, those with women at the helm had fared "systematically and significantly better" than their patriarchal counterparts.' Female leaders have leaned more towards truth and compassion, also demonstrating incredible decisiveness in dealing with lockdowns and measures to block the virus spread. There were no political games or power plays; only a vested interest in keeping the country and its inhabitants as safe as possible. It has allowed us to see what women are capable of when under pressure.

Dealing with pressure comes with a powerful emotional element: for a long time, being emotional has been seen as a negative with regards to women, especially in the work environment—but what if being emotional is exactly the key to being a great leader? Instead of trying to be 'one of the guys', why not embrace our emotional side and learn to use it to our advantage? Our instincts come from an emotional place, and so learning to trust our instincts and lead with compassion could do a wealth of good.

As stated by Jude Kelly (artistic director of the Southbank Centre, UK), 'Women have to honour their potential. Women must give themselves the right to thrive in every single way, and not define how loving or humble they are by the amount that they are prepared to step sideways to accommodate someone else. They need to say, "I've got one life, I've been given life, it has been breathed into me, and here I am, and I should use it for the best possible purpose." Whatever each woman herself defines that to be.'

If being an inspiring leader is what you want to become, then you will find everything you need is already within you: you can create the impact you want by increasing your self-awareness of how you want to be and who you want to be and by working with purpose and belief. The more aware we are, the more deliberate we can be about our intentions, and our impact will be greater. Our impact, in turn, will inspire others to embrace their power. Don't just be ambitious for yourself; be ambitious for the women around you. Support each other, mentor each other, and grow together. Brita Fernandez Schmidt said, 'As I witness another woman's rising, she gives me wings.'

I love working with female leaders, helping them to find their purpose within their role and inspiring them to inspire others, creating a community for them to find true mentorship and guidance through the tough moments, helping women find the innate power within them that they have lost touch with and helping them to stand up for themselves at work and find better ways of communicating to improve performance throughout their team and beyond. The barriers women face in climbing the leadership ladder will not go away overnight, but together, we can break them down and show the world what female leadership looks like.

Until next time, I encourage you to listen to your inner power, because *you* are the change.

Contact Elizabeth

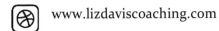 www.lizdaviscoaching.com

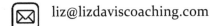 liz@lizdaviscoaching.com

in Liz Davis

ROCHELLE GILBURN

Gilburn Investment Group founder, completing house sales in as little as two weeks for those looking to find the right properly

A TRAUMATIC EVENT CAN MAKE or break you.

When my husband passed away suddenly in 2018, it brought around the realisation that life is too short; that it shouldn't be wasted; that I should go on to live my life to the fullest—not only for my husband but for myself and our two children.

I came from a deprived area in Sheffield and saw my mum and dad constantly struggling for money. We went to a great school on the other side of

Sheffield, my parents paying for me to attend martial arts classes. Like all parents, they wanted to make sure that we had a good life, despite our financial difficulties.

My parents split up when I was six years old. My dad had his house repossessed at one point, and my mum got stung by negative equity after the 2008 recession and had to sell her house and start renting instead.

Balancing keeping up with the Jones' and getting out of debt was a massive struggle for them. I can remember thinking, *If only my mum and dad were still together... We would have plenty of money.*

I'd always been ambitious as a child: I set my goals high and went for them. I knew that I didn't want to struggle like my parents had. Hence, I started babysitting at fourteen so that I could afford to go to the cinema or out for a meal with my friends without having to ask my parents for more money. When I got a job at sixteen, I would take extra hours and get temporary jobs over the summer. I knew I wanted to go places and provide my children with the life my parents had wanted for me, without the financial pressures.

But then, I let life get in the way: I got a part-time job, got a boyfriend, and had kids—and before I knew it, I'd worked at the same place for fourteen years and lost sight of my goals and dreams. Don't get me wrong, I still worked hard, and my husband had a good job, so money wasn't an issue, and I was fully able to provide for my children; but even still, I lost that fire in my belly. I no longer had big dreams. I wasn't unhappy, but I wasn't fulfilling my potential, either.

And there's nothing like a traumatic event to shake up a mundane life and make you realise how short life is!

My husband passed away suddenly in October 2018.

Initially, I was left with emptiness: my life was completely up in the air, and I lost my sense of purpose. However, instead of letting it break me, it set me on a path of self-discovery. I had to relearn who I was—no longer a wife but a single mum to a two- and four-year-old, the sole breadwinner for a family.

I knew I had two choices: let the grief eat away at me, or use the grief to fire me up.

Whenever I sat around doing nothing, the grief was unbearable, so I went back to work after six weeks—but it wasn't the same: I had worked with my husband, and it was noticeable that he wasn't there. Besides, I was no longer challenged by the job, and I found myself becoming depressed. I knew I had to do something about it.

The next stage of my grief made me a bit of a party animal—a coping mechanism. I went on weekend breaks to Iceland, Amsterdam, and Vegas, as well as a ream of festivals. I needed things in life to look forward to. The future looked scarily big and empty, so I had to create milestones for myself.

I ended up leaving my job in the search of something more, ultimately taking some time out to find myself. I spent time at the gym, having coffees with friends and managing to keep myself busy—but I knew I was capable of more, and I *wanted* more.

I'd been speaking to a good friend who was in property, and considering I'd inherited a bit of money, I thought building a property portfolio might be a good distraction. However, the more I talked to her, the more I was inspired to set up my own property business. Hence, I started to educate myself and completed a property course— something I never expected to send me on the journey that it has. What started as me wanting to dabble in a bit of property turned into me running a successful property business, inspiring other property professionals to grow their businesses, as well as encouraging people to get started with investing in property.

My business is about so much more than just

property. I love property, but what I love more is the freedom that it can give you.

Let me explain my business model to you. I am firstly a marketer, meaning I find properties and investors before bringing the two together. The investor buys the property and I manage the process right through to letting out the property. I also invest in property myself and look for investors to invest in my property business. (I'll give you more information about this later on!)

When I stumbled into property, I'd been looking for a job that allowed me the flexibility to be able to spend time with my children, do the school run, and do my hobbies, such as go to the gym, do martial arts, and have the odd pamper session. I was fed up with the restrictions a job puts on me, and there were limited part-time jobs available, which mean a step backwards. Running out of options, I looked for full-time jobs, despite knowing I'd have to put my children in childcare. This bothered me greatly: they'd already lost one parent, and I wanted to make sure I was as present as possible.

Starting my business made sense, and as a result of it, I've been able to do the school run, fit in time for my hobbies, and still build a business that is going places; I can work during the evening or at weekends and have the general flexibility to ensure that I have an amazing work-life balance.

I want to give that back to others. Not everyone has the freedom to set up a business, but they may have money in the bank that could create a passive income for themselves.

I want to advise and inspire people to do more with their money in a way that will give them financial freedom, allow them to spend more time with their family, and retire that bit earlier.

I also love the other side of my business: unfortunately, people do find themselves in financial difficulty, and like my parents, they may find that they can no longer afford their homes. The worst-case scenario is that their house gets repossessed and they end up in debt—but what if a company like mine could come in and buy it in a matter of weeks, in turn freeing them from that financial burden and giving them enough money to start their life all over again? Whilst I am a business owner and the aim of a business is clearly to generate money, I love to offer a win-win-win situation for my clients: I want the person selling their house to walk away happy, feeling like they have got a good deal and a weight has been lifted off their shoulders; I want the investor buying the property to feel like they are getting a good deal that will benefit their family for generations to come; and I obviously want to feel like I have won in helping two families have a better life whilst helping mine at the same time.

I am creating a legacy for my family. This is about more than property; it's about getting out of a poverty cycle, providing for my children and their children, giving back to my parents, and inspiring other people to ensure that their families have the best life.

One of the things I have loved most about my journey so far is that I have inspired people. We all have problems in life, and for me, one of the things I am proudest of is that when life knocks me down, I make sure I stand straight back up. I am a big believer in the fact that it's not what happens to us but how we *deal* with it that counts.

Mindset is so important, and building a strong foundation for this has helped me to cope with the loss of my husband, ultimately keeping me going. Of course, there are days when everything gets too much and I wonder why I am doing this, but then I focus back on my 'why'—my husband, my children, and myself. I want to be able to look back on my life and know that I made the most of it. We are only here once, and I don't want to let fear, sadness, negativity, or self-doubting beliefs hold me back.

Of course I want to make money, but the most important thing to me is that I am inspiring and encouraging people to live a fulfilling life; to fight through the pains and misfortune and know that they can have more.

A lot of the people I talk to have wanted to get involved in property for years, and they have the money sat there in the bank. The only thing that is stopping them is the obstacles that are in the way. The three most common obstacles are time, knowledge, and fear. My clients are usually busy professionals who love their jobs and have no intention of going full-time in property; they just want to invest their money into something that will give them a good return, and yet they have no time to look for opportunities to educate themselves on the market.

A story I hear quite often is that a person has spent hours on their day off looking for property opportunities, during which they booked in a whole day's worth of viewings for their next day off—but by the time viewing day arrives, the majority of the properties have already been sold. If they are lucky enough to find a property, organising trades is a nightmare, especially for those who live in the south of England and are looking to buy in the north for the strong yields. They don't know anyone in the area, so who can they trust?

Indeed, a lot of clients feel like they don't know enough about property to risk investing large sums of money into it; instead, they need someone to hold their hand and guide them through it.

Meanwhile, others are just scared: is it the right time to invest? What if I buy wrong? What if the housing market crashes? Is that the right area? Am I paying the right price? They have so many questions in their mind that they end up talking themselves out of it, and ten years later, they are still thinking about investing in property and wishing they'd done it when prices were lower, before they had kids, or when they got that inheritance. We often let excuses and beliefs get in our way and hold us back.

I offer my clients a hands-free property investment service. Some of my clients are looking to build a portfolio of houses that will give them cash flow into their retirement; others want a completely hands-off service and invest money with my business to generate an annual return on their investment. Either way, finding the right property can be difficult and time-consuming, especially in an upward market—which is what we are currently in! My clients tell me that they try to find properties through the traditional methods, but they are selling too quickly or going for way more than their actual value. In line with this, the advantages of working with me are as follows.

- **Time.** I am full-time in this business and have people working for me. Hence, we are able to view hundreds of houses, put in hundreds of offers, and get offers accepted in a time-efficient way.
- **Network.** I have invested a lot of time in building up relationships with key people in the property industry. When you are known for being in property, people start to bring you opportunities!
- **Marketing.** There are two sides to my business: finding investors and finding houses for investors to buy. I have over ten years of experience in marketing and use that to find the best property deals through my company Sell Your House South Yorkshire. This gives me access to properties that are not on the property market; nearly forty thousand homes that sold in 2020 were off-market!

Doing the right things every day that create momentum and drive the business forward is paramount, and I love that my clients keep coming back for more as a result of this consistency. Whilst I am always taking on new investors, as soon as I find an investor for a property, if they have the funds, they want me to find the next one. It's always rewarding to know that people are so happy with your services that they want to continue to work with you and also recommend you to others!

The first investor that I signed was an experienced investor who used other property professionals to find him properties, but they had stopped bringing him anything due to the market; they were struggling to find the deals. After coming to me, I found him two within a short period, and he is now asking for a third one.

When people are investing their life savings into property, trust is so important—and because of this, I love that I am building relationships for the long term. I'm not just looking to make a quick buck and move on!

People who are selling their houses come to me for various reasons, whether that be financial, divorce-related, or concerned with moving abroad. However, one story that stands out to me is one of an eighty-year-old man who was moving in with his eighty-year-old girlfriend: he'd collected a house packed full of belongings, and she told him that he could only bring a couple of bags. He wanted a quick and easy sale where he didn't have to worry about sorting through his five hundred and sixty-four videos or his jars of marbles. He took what was important to him and the tradesmen sorted out the rest.

Another story that stands out is one where a couple had split up, the lady staying in the family home with two children, unable to afford the bills. She put her house on the market and got offered a council house. She couldn't afford to keep both houses while the sale went through the traditional conveyancing process, so she reached out to my company and my investor bought the property in cash. This meant she could move into her council house straight away without getting caught up in a chain and having to pay for two sets of bills.

I get real satisfaction knowing that I have solved someone's property problem and am helping them to move on with their life smoothly. I've also provided my investor with a fantastic rental property for his portfolio!

My Offers

Portfolio Building
Here, I'll give you advice on what kind of properties and strategies would give you the return you need to live the life you want. I will hold your hand through

the process and will go out, find you a property to meet your requirements, and give you access to my team of solicitors, mortgage brokers, tax advisers, and accountants. I'll manage the process right through to the sale and get my team of builders in to do any necessary refurbishment to the property and get it rental-ready. I'll then put you in touch with a recommended letting agency.

Fixed Returns

With interest rates so low these days, a great alternative to leaving money in the bank is to invest it wisely for a fixed annual return. Here, I'll go out and invest your money into my property projects, where I'll buy, renovate, and sell on the properties. I will then give you an annual fixed return on your money.

Contact Rochelle

Property is a very male-dominated space, and I would *love* to work with more female investors! If you've been thinking about investing in property, I would love to chat. Reach out to me via LinkedIn or my website www.gilburninvestmentgroup.com and we can organise a no-obligation phone call to discuss your circumstances and how I can help you build a passive income through property.

 www.rochellegilburn.com/invest-in-property

 www.facebook.com/rochellegilburn

 www.linkedin.com/in/Rochelle-Gilburn

LAYLA HINCHEN

Winning PMU Artist & Trainer, delivering education and support on-demand for clients everywhere

A MUM AT NINETEEN, SINGLE by twenty-one, and paying my mortgage on a credit card just to keep a roof over our heads, it's safe to say that I didn't make things easy for myself.

I had a great childhood. We weren't wealthy by any means, but my mum and dad both worked hard to ensure that we didn't want for anything; we had nice holidays every year, went on lots of trips during the school holidays, and all-around had a very decent upbringing.

I had it all mapped out: I started my A-Levels at college in biology, chemistry, English, and psychology, and I was going to go to university to do marine biology—following in my brother's footsteps. During college, I landed a part-time job, got used to earning money, and ended up not completing my second year of school. I loved working, and I realised that the university route wasn't for me. It was a tough choice—I didn't want to disappoint my family—, but I knew that it wasn't what I wanted to do.

I was working in accounting in the city on what was great pay for me at the time, being only eighteen—but after around six months, I hated it, sitting at the same desk day in and day out, seeing the same people and spreadsheets. I dreaded that train commute every morning. I had had a few temporary jobs before this, and after a few months, I would always move onto the next job; it was easy back then to walk out of one office and into a new one the day after. I couldn't settle anywhere: office life just wasn't for me, quite clearly. Had I messed up my chances by dropping out of college? The regret started to flood in very quickly.

Then, along came my little surprise: I was pregnant! My partner and I hadn't been trying, so this was a big shock. I'll never forget the tears running down my mum's face when I told her, terrified to tell my dad and brother. I could feel their pure disappointment in me. Everyone told me that I had thrown my life away, including my friends—but why? Why did this have to mean I wouldn't make anything of my life? Everyone suddenly looking down on me just made me more determined to not let this be the end of my career!

We got a council flat in a high rise in Bethnal Green, East London—not the nicest of areas to be in, but what mattered was that we had our own flat. Getting verbally abused each time I had to pass the gangs on the stairs just became normality to me very quickly; carrying the pram and shopping up eight flights of stairs each time the lift was out of order proved to keep me nice and fit. Life wasn't peachy—I suffered quite badly with post-natal depression at this point, sobbing all day whilst my son was in his cot also crying—, but I was making do with what I had.

It was when I was at one of my lowest points that my mum to the rescue; she had spotted this and talked me straight into seeing the doctor. A few months later, I started to feel like myself again. My mum then offered to help us to buy a house and get out of where we were. I will forever be grateful for this opportunity, and I fully acknowledge and appreciate how lucky I was. So we did: we bought our first maisonette in Essex at the age of twenty. Life was looking up. I left my city job and went back to college in the evenings, doing a beauty therapy NVQ. I didn't see this as my long-term career; rather, it was a means for me to earn enough money to get by until I decided what I really wanted to do workwise. Even though I was now a mum at nineteen, I had every intention of working.

Six months later, I found out my partner was having an affair, and we separated. He left and offered no support at all—not a penny towards the mortgage or our son. So, there I was, twenty and with a one-year-old, trying to pay a mortgage with only about £150 - £200 a month from the beauty treatments I was doing here and there. As each month passed, my mountain of debt grew: credit cards were stacking up. I was determined not to lose this house after I'd been given the opportunity to take such a huge step in life. I wasn't going to struggle anymore or feel sorry for myself; I needed to take action—and so my first business was born. I was out leaflet-dropping, putting ads in shop windows, and offering anyone I knew a referral discount, doing whatever I could to get some clients and make a full-time job of it. This beauty could no longer serve me as 'pocket money'; I needed a real income, and I couldn't survive on credit forever. We didn't have Facebook and Instagram at this point, nor any of the other amazing platforms we have today, and so it was the good old yellow pages and directories that I used to advertise.

With a lot of hard work and dedication, my mobile beauty business took off. I was so lucky to have support from my mum with my son whilst I was working.

After just a few months, I was no longer paying my mortgage on a credit card: I was doing it on my own—and what's more, I was enjoying it! I didn't dread going to work; I loved working. As the money started coming in and I started clearing my debt, my passion for business grew: being my own boss, working my own hours (kinda!), and making a decent living was a dream, and I had a hunger for more.

In the evenings, I'd study business and marketing via any course I could find so I could learn how to grow. I also started doing more beauty courses and adding to my services, and I also converted my mum's garage at her house into a beauty room. I didn't have to go mobile anymore; I was working from there, my own little setup.

As my son started school, my hours increased, my marketing was working, and my business was growing. I would work during school hours and then in the evenings, once he was in bed. I was approached by a private company I had trained with and was asked if I would be interested in teaching for them. I jumped at the opportunity: I loved helping others and had recently been doing a bit of requested mentoring. Hence, I went straight onto the next available PTTLS (now AET) course for teaching.

I had finally found my passion in life: I fell in love with teaching. Helping others and watching them succeed brought so much fulfilment to me. Permanent makeup became my focus—a treatment I absolutely thrive off of doing—, so combining this with teaching meant that I had finally found my perfect career. I still offer clinics alongside teaching, as I just love helping men and women; the confidence these treatments bring to people is so rewarding. It's not just makeup!

I then also went on to train in 3D areola tattooing, helping women (and men) post-mastectomy following breast cancer. This was an important step in my journey and something I had always wanted to offer. I run free clinics for this treatment every month, waiting until I was in a position to be able to do this for free before offering the service, as I knew I didn't want to charge for it;

sometimes, it's nice just to be able to give a little back.

It was hard work juggling everything, but it was doable. As the teaching side grew, so did the rest of the business. For years, I toyed with the idea of opening my own salon, but every time I looked at the overheads I bottled it, staying put in my home salon. I always knew that I would get there one day—it was a goal in life—, but I had to do it when the time was right.

However, it turns out that the time was never right. This is one thing I wish I had dared to do sooner.

In 2016, I got to a point where I couldn't cope on my own anymore: my diary was booked months ahead and I was having to turn clients away daily. I knew it was time. I was now pregnant with my daughter, and I could have easily talked myself back out of the commitment of juggling a clinic with a newborn—but if I knew that if I didn't proceed with this, I wouldn't have the ability to continue to grow.

I signed there and then at the first place I looked at: I knew it was perfect for what I wanted, and it just felt right. Since then, the business has gone from strength to strength, and in January 2021, we moved into a larger building with a high street front. My final goal for the clinic and I was to finally have my name above the door—and, indeed, what once had been a dream that seemed so far off became a reality. I now have a team of seven amazing ladies, and we continue to grow each year.

Sometimes, we use bad timing as an excuse for our fears; to not follow our dreams. However, I truly don't think there ever is a right time: if you have a goal and you want to move towards it, sometimes, you have to take risks. Get out of your comfort zone. For me, over the years, I have learnt to trust my gut and just go for it. After all, what's the worst that could happen? I'd much rather try and fail than not try at all!

I was fortunate with my childhood, and I wanted to make sure my children never wanted for anything. I have always wanted to be able to set them up for life in the same way that my mum helped me with moving out—and now, I own another two flats which will be theirs one day, when they are ready. It hasn't been easy—I have struggled and worked myself into the ground—, but having that end vision and goal in place helped me to push through to where I am now. Anyone is capable of achieving their dreams; you just need to believe in yourself and go for it.

As I delved further into business and we got busier and busier, I hit a stage more recently where it took over my life: I no longer had time to see friends or family; I was always too busy. I never slept and couldn't switch off. I felt like I had gone back to square one in my end goal, the life I had worked so hard to build kind of slipping away. Now, all I did was work again, 24/7.

I then started working with some business and life coaches who helped me to find balance in life again. I discovered that mindset was a huge part of entrepreneurship and that having that work-life balance was crucial. I guess business can become addictive. It did for me, anyway! Always chasing, getting that thrill when you reach a goal, setting yourself bigger goals and bigger challenges. Now, don't get me wrong, setting goals and aiming for growth is good—but you also need a reality check sometimes to refocus and remember what is more important in the long run.

My second long-term relationship broke down at this point, and one of the main reasons for this was my work: I was always too busy, only focused on and interested in work, too tired for anything else— and whilst my business was thriving, my home life was suffering. I couldn't see it at the time—I blamed him for being unsupportive—, but looking back with a clearer mind, I can see just how difficult I must have been to live with: I worked so hard to be able to have a good income and enjoy freedom with my family that I lost my vision along the way. Being an entrepreneur can be a rollercoaster of a ride: we learn as we go; we make mistakes. It's part of growth, and because of this, it's important to take time out to reflect and learn from these mistakes.

I have grown a lot as an individual as well as a business over the years; I am still working on that life balance, but I now always ensure I keep it as my main focus before I end up burned out. I have the security I need behind me to not have any financial worries, and I purposefully block time out in my diary so I can maintain that freedom to go on holidays, spend quality time with my family, keep a bit more of a balance, and have a career that I love. The risks paid off, and I know now that I am on the right path for me.

Running a business is hard work, but it is also so rewarding. Forget the work-your-own-hours excitement that is prevalent in the beginning; I think I was pretty much working 24/7 either physically or on the business side of things the whole time! Being a sole trader brings many hats to wear: you're the owner, accountant, marketing department, customer service, the service/product itself... It's a juggle! It can also be quite lonely, especially if you don't have anyone close with the same mindset and goals in life as you; someone to look at things from your perspective; to bounce ideas off of; to bring you back down to earth. People don't always understand these struggles and how they can consume you if they are not entrepreneurs.

I wish I had discovered business and life coaches much earlier on in my journey. My personal life may have been very different to how it is now if I had! But hey, it's all been a learning curve, and maybe this is how my story was meant to go. Regardless, it was because of this that I went on to create The PMU Circle. As a permanent makeup artist, we generally work alone— no one to bounce ideas off; no one to ask when you're second-guessing your choices (unless you pay around £1,000 per day for further mentoring!); no one to help you with your business. We are all taught how to offer these services but rarely do training courses that help you to actually run a business. I learnt the hard way, via trial-and-error, and because of this, it took me much longer to reach this point than it needed to.

I don't want other artists to have the same struggles that I did. Hence, we have created an amazing community of friendly and supportive artists, helping in all aspects of permanent makeup and business. The permanent makeup industry is no longer a lonely place, and it is amazing to watch how everyone is coming together and supporting each other! Collaboration over competition all day long. Together, we can all help to raise the standards in the industry and make it a beautiful, much safer place for new artists now coming into it.

The PMU Circle Pro is a monthly subscription platform, where a brand-new educational module is delivered to the artists' platforms every single month. From as little as £25 per month, artists can further their education, ensure they are working safely, network, and gain support—without the huge costs usually associated with permanent makeup training. In this way, artists gain confidence much more quickly and can successfully grow their careers.

The feedback we get from our members is mind-blowing; I have to pinch myself each day! What started as a little idea when having a casual chat with my team is now being recognised as one of the biggest platforms in the permanent makeup industry.

It was my PA, Katie, who came up with this idea. She was going through my Facebook messages when she brought it to my attention that I had many messages from artists I had never trained reaching out to me for support. We threw some ideas around with Claire, who I work very closely with—and so

The PMU Circle was born! The logo was designed that night and the pre-launch posted straight on social media. I wanted to get the idea out there immediately and see what interest it gained!

Well, it's safe to say that I was a little shocked when we had over one hundred people sign up pretty much instantly. Despite my excitement, this posed a problem: I now had signups with absolutely no content ready to go. However, this ended up serving as a good motivator for me. I got straight to work.

This instant popularity just went to show how many artists were out there with zero support from their trainers after parting with thousands and thousands and how this was such a big gap in our industry! The platform allowed me to help artists from all over the world and to bring them together.

Getting feedback from members on how much they have grown since finding us and how they may have given up on their dream if they hadn't come across The PMU Circle is one of my biggest highlights ever; it is what drives me to keep pushing forward and growing the platform. We want to be able to help as many people as possible.

When I entered the industry, it was a very lonely place: no one was willing to help you post-training, as everyone saw everybody else as competition. It was quite a hostile place to be. Hence, it is so rewarding seeing that change! So many trainers now are much more open and willing to help and share. As a group effort, we are making those changes.

Whether through The PMU Circle, the artist development program (our detailed online learning for existing artists), or our hands-on beginner's training here in Essex, our mission is to ensure that artists are equipped with the tools and support they need not just to succeed, but excel in their careers.

We have lots of free content on our YouTube channel @thepmucircle and a free Facebook group with over three thousand artists offering their advice and support. If you are considering starting a career in permanent makeup or you are an existing artist looking to further your skills and gain additional support, please do reach out to us on social media or via email!

Contact Layla

 www.laylahinchen.com

www.facebook.com/laylahinchenpmu

Facebook Group: The PMU Circle

www.instagram.com/laylahinchen

www.instagram.com/thepmucircle

ZINA KULAR

Body & Business Confidence Coach & owner of Zina Kular Coaching, helping women to burst out of their boxes and reimagine the life they have always wanted

ALTHOUGH I CAME FROM A family of small business owners, I was not expected to become an entrepreneur. I was privately educated because my family wanted the future for me that they never had: sixth form, university, and getting a secure, reputable job was the expectation. And I did exactly that: I got a degree and qualified as a secondary school maths teacher.

As any teacher knows, teaching is not just a job; it's a lifestyle. I embraced this and very quickly got promoted to mid-management. I soon found myself covering for any teacher shortages, working twelve or more hours a day just to keep up with my workload and bringing work home at the weekends. I didn't have time to eat most days, so between eight and twelve cups of coffee usually kept me going, and then I would inhale whatever came in sight once I got home. Naturally, this meant I was constantly falling ill and experienced burnout often. However, I felt like I was making such a positive difference to the lives of the students that I convinced myself that my health could be a focus for a later date, when I had spare time.

Of course, the 'spare time' never came up, and so I would just power through, burn out, and repeat.

The turning point for me was when my mum was diagnosed with cancer. At this news, my world fell apart. It was also then that I realised that this world in which I already felt stretched was demanding more from me, and so I decided then and there to leave teaching and spend more time with my mum whilst figuring out what to do with my career.

Meanwhile, my mum refused to let the diagnosis determine her quality of life and did whatever she could to make the most of the time she had left in this world. Through the journey that my mum went on, I learned so much about health, self-care, positive energy, and healing methods. By looking after her own health, nutrition, energy, mindset, and spirituality, my mum managed to extend her life expectancy from six months to three years—and *that* remains the most powerful first-hand experience I have ever witnessed. It struck a chord in me that I had never felt before, and I was suddenly inspired to help people with their health holistically—but first, I knew that the work on myself had only just begun.

My parents had grafted hard in their lives as they dreamt of creating the best retirement for themselves. I was brought up with the money mindset of saving for a better future so that I could truly enjoy myself once I was retired. This never sat well with me, and I would always question why we couldn't spend money on the things we loved *now*. To this, I would always get the same response: 'Save your money for a rainy day. You never know what's around the corner!' This made me feel selfish for wanting to buy things for myself, especially when considering the fact that my mum rarely treated herself to things without giving it an immense amount of thought. A true discomfort around money crept up in me consistently, and I carried this baggage through to my adult life. Of course, what was around the corner was so unexpected for us that when my mum passed away and I saw how my parents' dreams of life after retirement shattered, I vowed to live a fulfilled life and create abundance *now*; to enjoy every moment we have in the present moment whilst still working towards a great future; to always pursue my dreams, no matter how bizarre they may seem to others. All of a sudden, there were so many shifts for me in my money mindset and my view of life; it's as if the Universe had opened up to me the endless possibilities that I just hadn't noticed before.

These lessons were just the beginning of my journey to where I am now. I worked on channelling the right energy, nutrition, and exercise to help my physical confidence. Then, I decided to work more on my mental and spiritual side. I immersed myself in each area I focused on until I felt that I had mastered it—not only for the present moment but also for its future evolutions.

Meanwhile, I fell into a corporate career and also started a side business in health. My job paid my bills and funded my lifestyle; my business fuelled my passion to help others. Both of these enhanced my skills and core personal development. Ultimately, my fascination with mindset and helping others attracted me to qualifying as a master practitioner in NLP, Timeline Therapy, and Hypnotherapy. The importance of looking after myself in order to deliver my absolute best in the world to fulfil my purpose was becoming established one step at a time as if the pieces of a puzzle were fitting together. This was by no means an easy journey, and the unlearning was more challenging at times than the learning—yet this was an essential part of my growth as a person.

Naturally, my most inspiring life lessons also came from my mum's attitude through life and then later through dealing with cancer. My mum was an amazing woman: she took on everything she physically could and dealt with them solo most of the time. I was amazed by her strength and how she always brought out the best in others.

However, I also witnessed the side of my mum that would absorb negativity from others. She was a problem solver, and this often took its toll from a mental health perspective, although she would never portray this to the outside world. There were a lot of compromises my mum made throughout life that really impacted her self-worth as a person, and she would often share these deeper reflections with me: she felt that she hadn't treated her body with the respect it deserved. After having me, she had done everything possible to conceive again, and after no results for ten years, she stopped trying—and then went on to have both of my brothers. On reflection, she felt that she had abused her body for those ten years and thought that she maybe could have conceived earlier if she had just learnt to love her body and felt gratitude rather than resentment and desperation.

Maybe these thoughts contributed to her cancerous cells being triggered. Regardless, it was during these moments of listening to my mum's reflections that the penny dropped for me: I needed to focus on loving my body, and only then would I be able to work *with* it and achieve what I wanted to in the world. It did not need to be a battle, which was how I had treated it until this moment. In my younger years, I had fallen victim to yo-yo dieting and having self-image and body confidence issues— so first, I had to forgive myself for the abuse I had put my body through. I realised how every area of my life had been (and was still being) affected by this negative self-image and lack of confidence. Hence, through working on loving myself, I experienced how powerful the mind and body connection is, and I began stepping into my true authentic self; I knew this was the only way to deliver my best to the world.

In my job and my business, I started noticing some people promoting the 'fake it till you make it' approach. I very quickly started realising how most of these people also had a negative bank balance or weren't earning as much as they were making out to be. Having learnt that we are all the average of the five people that we surround ourselves with, I was adamant that I was going to find a more inspiring crowd of people to surround myself with in business; that I wouldn't have another year in business being guided by *anyone* who promoted this way of life since it was not only negative and shrinking me as a person, but I was spending a lot of energy keeping up this fake façade only to break even in business. For me, this didn't just mean no money; it told me that I wasn't making much of an impact in the world, and I wasn't making as much of a difference as I would have liked to have been. Hence, it was at this time that I started really questioning my purpose in business—and ultimately, I decided to make a change, as I had learnt a lot of lessons about how I *didn't* want to do business. Now, it was time to do it *my* way—a way that made me feel empowered rather than wanting to hide away.

In line with this revelation, I started practising being genuine with myself and my customers: I started listening better and tuning in to how I could make the biggest impact on people's lives without focusing so much on the outcome or what others thought of me and my image. 'Marry the process; divorce the outcome' was a motto I had heard often but not understood or seen in practice—until now. I became attracted to people who would show their struggles in business; those who would talk about how they overcame their difficulties and succeeded throughout them. I started networking better to find these people, following them on social media and reading books about mindset, purpose, success, and breakthroughs—and then I practised. It felt scary to show my vulnerabilities, and through it, I received messages and feedback from so many others saying they were inspired by my journey so far. I knew I had people watching me for being authentically me, and that felt amazing! These people were accepting me, scars and all, and I was showing up better, being real and making a real effort to step into my genuine self. My clients started to see this, too: I had doubled my sales targets in my corporate job and made more sales in my business, attracting so many more valuable business associates and expanding my network with truly inspirational people that I was learning from every day. I achieved so much more in this year than I had ever done before, despite devastatingly losing my mum and going through a miscarriage that very same year. I do not doubt that all the work I did on my body confidence, self-image, and mindset truly helped me to deal with the year, as I was not only able to get through it all and come out of the other end, but I did so stronger—and I was able to be there for others, too! It became blatantly obvious that nobody could operate on an empty vessel, and you certainly cannot show up authentically for your clients in business without looking after yourself first. I had experienced my first real breakthrough during the most traumatic year of my life, and I was so grateful for it. Thus, my passion to help others to become wealthy and live the life of their dreams through being their authentic selves in business was born.

My vision is to encourage and empower women to be their true, authentic selves; to be real and embrace their uniqueness, scars and all. I see a world where business owners are stepping into their purpose and owning it. I am fascinated by the power of women in business and the female Shakti that rises from within! She is magnanimous, and we need to learn to channel her to help deliver our purpose in life. I have seen it, felt it, and experienced it—a unique brilliance that lives within all of us.

I have always believed that people's realities are determined by the choices they make in life, and so if I was unhappy with my situation, that I should make a change. However, the problem was I would change direction a little too often: I was spontaneous, and at the time, it worked for me. However, this was mostly my way of seeking adjustment—yet my actions would often lead me to a complete change of direction. I was forced to change this approach when I started my own family: I had to incorporate a better structure and think about so many other factors before making drastic changes, as naturally, it would affect my small family in big ways.

Motherhood took me from spontaneous to rigidly structured, and this didn't come naturally to me: I was brought up in a South-Asian family where there was an open-door policy—and I had married into one, too—, meaning that anyone could turn up at our house at any time and they would always be invited in for a cup of tea and catch up—no call in advance; no pre-warning.

The same was expected of me as a daughter and daughter-in-law, and so when it came to working from home, there were boundaries to be established here. Since my way of working wasn't understood by many, it also wasn't respected, and therefore more expectations would be put on me. It took some resilience, determination, and decisions my husband

and I had to make in setting boundaries for us to create a different future for ourselves. When you have self-respect, your expectation of yourself is what matters the most over anyone else's. My journey has not been understood (and still isn't) by many despite proving repeatedly that I am living a much more fulfilled life now than I ever have done before, and I know I am not alone in this experience. My best advice in this case would be to always be true to yourself: always uphold your morals and never compromise on what you are building to entertain the limitations of what others think that you cannot achieve. I recognise now that my job isn't to convince anyone to understand my journey, but to live a fulfilled life and be content with my own decisions. I'm sure most of us have heard the quote 'your vibe attracts your tribe', and it is so true! Not everyone will understand you, and not everyone will understand your journey, but as long as you know that you are making progress towards your goals, that is what matters the most. The rest will fall into pace effortlessly.

Time is precious. I know this from my mum's journey, and I was also learning this very quickly in business. It took some experimenting and investing in myself through self-development courses and mastermind days, and it took adjusting and readjusting before I found a balance that worked for me. With every significant life event that occurred—having a baby, moving house, changing job—I had to readjust, reschedule, and recalibrate. It wasn't easy, and because I was so rigid with my schedule, I would feel stressed at the thought of having to adjust everything again: I would go from juggling one area of life to another, and ultimately whichever area of life I wasn't focusing on in that moment would come crumbling down. I operated on an 'all or nothing' type mentality and then faced burnout—repeatedly.

This was not my idea of living a fulfilled life, and I had a lightbulb moment when a mentor said to me, 'The most successful people are the most flexible in their approach to business.' This was another penny-drop moment for me: I stopped over-planning and under-achieving, as it was shattering my sense of accomplishment, and I became kinder to myself, starting instead to focus on and listen to my body and what it was capable of. The shift from constantly feeling like I was falling short of my goals to absolutely conquering my daily, weekly, and monthly tasks was incredible. It demonstrated how by letting go, you can achieve so much more.

As all successful business owners do, I also experienced many pain points along the way, and the above are just some of the hurdles I have crossed. It took me years to work on strategies for myself and to get them right, and that was mainly due to my identifying and finding my way through the façade of fake entrepreneurship to find what was real and what I could honestly see myself comfortably doing for the long term. My mission is to make this effortless for all who I work with; to help busy female entrepreneurs to align their business and life goals, leverage their time, and increase their income, helping them to unleash their inner lioness and let out their roar.

I have combined my years of experience, knowledge, reading, strategies, and tips to ensure that anyone who works with me can avoid the mistakes that I made along the way and accelerate their success at speed. I have combined all of these elements into a mentorship programme that helps female entrepreneurs to fall in love with themselves to show up better for their clients. When female entrepreneurs first approach me, they have typically begun feeling frustrated with their business because it has not quite scaled to where they would have liked it to, the reason for this being that they entered the world of entrepreneurship for reasons all entrepreneurs may relate to: work-life balance, uncapped income, control over the decisions and ethics of the company, flexible working hours, etc. However, they are at a point where life has become busier and they feel that in order to expand their business, they'll need to dedicate more time to the business—more than what they would ideally like to be doing long-term. Usually, they've been feeling a little deflated and stretched in life generally. They know it shouldn't feel like this and want to avoid resenting what they've built up so far. As a result, they are not as in control of other areas of life such as body image goals and feel that they aren't as present as they should be with loved ones. There is a deep sense of dissatisfaction permeating their life, yet they can't pinpoint it—or don't know where to start. There are just too many things to do and think of—something that is starting to get picked up on by clients, too, as they just haven't been as visible online and on their platforms as much as they have been before (or as much as they would ideally like to be in order to achieve the results they want).

Upon completing the mentorship with my help, these amazing ladies can learn strategies and apply skills that have enabled them to step into the best version of themselves; they are able to authentically and unapologetically unleash their inner lioness and their roar. The strategies learnt through this programme will help them to become magnetic to their clients, and these same strategies often help them in the other areas of life that were becoming problem areas.

My dream goal for my clients is that they are able to burst out of this box that they have created around themselves and reimagine the life they have always wanted.

I also really enjoy speaking publicly about how body and business confidence are interlinked, and have spoken at networking events across the country at various events, such as National Women's Day. More frequently over the national lockdown, I have enjoyed speaking on podcasts and as a guest speaker for various group pages and memberships. This is a service I will continue to provide, as I am truly passionate about helping women to unlock their potential through the alignment of all their goals, authenticity, and achieving the life they truly desire. If my words can help just one person listening on the day, whether in person or otherwise, it's been worth it.

One of my biggest wins so far in business is to be able to authentically show up for my clients, unapologetically and abundantly. I went from being super nervous before every meeting to getting excited butterflies at the anticipation of changing the world working together with another amazing woman, one step at a time. This has not only come from changing my approach, applying my authenticity, getting clear on what I am delivering, and being real, but also from practice and feedback—and being noticed in my community via my clients and social media platforms is the icing on the cake for me!

Since stepping out of my comfort zone, I have demonstrated how so much more can be achieved by taking risks and pursuing dreams; I have shown that it's possible not only to be your own boss but to also be there for others. I have been able to be there for my family and take time off work when I want to; I have been present at family functions and celebrations, and am still the mum that is able to spend an endless amount of time and do many activities with my little boy—all whilst continuously expanding my business and outreach and growing my income. I have proudly been able to inspire friends to explore the world of entrepreneurship who had never considered it to be an option before, and some have said to me that that they have felt a sense of confidence watching my journey unfold before their eyes despite being so sceptical when I first started.

In the world I come from, it's unusual for someone who was so education-focused to leave a well-paid career behind to pursue what seemed like a gamble to others—and now, I have demonstrated that it can pay off tenfold! The abundance I feel and the passion that runs through my veins to encourage others to believe that it's possible for themselves keeps me motivated every single day; the power of sharing from the heart is immeasurable, motivation becomes effortless, and expansion becomes inevitable. The world really is your oyster!

If any of what I have spoken about so far has resonated with you, it would be my pleasure to invite you into my world of social media via my Facebook, Instagram, and LinkedIn. I love connecting personally with people. My favourite way of explaining entrepreneurship is that it begins with a wish, develops into a dream, and becomes a reality through grit, determination, and pursuit.

Like in any relationship, compatibility is essential. For anyone who would be keen to know how to work with me, I would like to offer a free discovery call to you. During this call, we would establish whether we are a good match for each other. I know that anyone who has booked a discovery call with me has always gone away with more value and determination than what they came with, and this is my guarantee, regardless of whether we end up working together in the future or not. As a special thank you for taking the time to read my chapter in this book, in addition to the discovery call, you will also receive a free PDF download (usually £90) with an exclusive step-by-step guide on Mindset Monkeys to Mindset Mastership', whereby you can master the art of mindset fatigue.

Thank you for allowing me to share my journey with you through this book. Until we meet again...

Contact Zina

 www.zinakular.com

 zina@zinakular.com

 Zina Kular

 www.instagram.com/zinakular

 Zina Kular

CAROLINE LECKEY

Business Coach & Mentor for recently separated women who are rebuilding their success

Sometimes the scariest bridge to burn is the one between you and the person you thought you were.
—Tanya Markul

WHAT DID I DO THE day it should have been my fifteenth wedding anniversary? I decided to take a huge leap into the known and write this chapter!

I am by no means a natural writer—more a thinker and talker—, but what I have now come to know for sure is that pain equals growth, and that stepping outside your comfort zone is huge. Being visible is one of my biggest fears, so deciding to go all-in on my fear was how I marked my first non-wedding anniversary!

Life is like a book full of chapters that we transition through, and what I have found is that my chapters often lack control from within: for me, making life changes started when I was a one-year-old and my family made a country move after my mum received the horrific news that both of her brothers had been killed in a tragic road traffic accident a few weeks before Christmas. There was a sense of loss and sadness that permeated my childhood from that point.

This was my first experience of how a lack of healing within the generation before you can trickle through and manifest as fresh wounds in you—and it is only when we stop and heal (or should I say self-heal) that we can fully appreciate the sheer strength that you find within when riding the wave of a life of transitions and the wounds that come with them. Periods of pain are, after all, periods of growth.

It took me forty-four years to pause and see this, and it took me forty-five to learn that you can self-heal. Life is a spectrum of colours from light to dark, and we must either embrace the full spectrum or choose not to at all.

It was in April 2020—one month into the pandemic lockdown—that I decided to hit pause and change almost every area of my life. Many female friends say I was brave in what followed, but the decision to be happy and figure out the 'how' was the turning point of years of feeling lost. On the outside, I of course looked confident, happy, educated, and successful, with a great career and family. All the boxes appeared ticked. However, in reality, I was lost, lonely, and unhappy, but wasn't sure why.

It was never my intention to have this 'anniversary of change'; rather, all that I knew was that standing still was not an option. Whilst I wasn't planning to do a leap of faith quite on this scale and to share my story (I am a very private person), I realised that I'd thus far not used the voice I'd been given, nor used the passion I felt, to help and support other women.

This revelation also helped me to realise that I was terrified to tap into myself; the truth was that I had been running from myself pretty much as far back as I could remember.

It was this realisation that made everything hit at once: I separated from a twenty-one-year relationship, fifteen of which I had been married for, and my world was swiftly turned upside-down as I moved country with two children and literally restarted my life, going back to square one by getting to know who I was. One of these events on its own is overwhelming enough, but instead, I rolled the dice and did all at once—with a global pandemic thrown in for good measure!

Not knowing myself was certainly one of the biggest challenges I faced; this tailspin of realising that I didn't was massively alarming. Don't get me wrong, on paper, it all looks very clear and logical in terms of my career history and the wins I have achieved along the way—but the CV had been the driving force with all of these ventures, not my true passions.

If there was ever a time when my emotions in all their rawness were going to appear in full force, it was most definitely going to be now. After all, what you don't realise when your marriage has failed is that there is going to be a spectrum of emotions that are going to emerge and take time to work through. The very word 'failed' is so heavy in and of itself, and adds another layer of guilt and shame on top of the other emotions that accompany such an event. This incredibly difficult decision was the first of many dominos to fall, and it also happened to be the start of me reconnecting and finding my way back to myself.

It takes one small step in life to create another life entirely. One step at a time is all that is needed; the 'how' will emerge if you believe in yourself and just focus on the next step.

The Seeds of Becoming a Woman of Influence

My passion has always been to nurture, help, sort, and fix everyone in my circle with regards taking their next step.

Throughout my career, I have always gravitated towards helping others, from making a real contribution within my community volunteering to simply standing up for the underdog. I am fortunate to have had a varied career history that I am very proud of, which ultimately led me to fulfil a goal I'd had for years: becoming a Professional Empowerment & Confidence Coach for women who have recently separated and are rebuilding their own success.

I grew up with the phrase 'it's a man's world' ingrained in my mindset—my much-loved nan said it to me frequently—and (maybe even counterintuitively) this has shaped my resilience and determinism to perform on par with men in the workplace. I have been exposed to strong male characters ever since I was a child, so you could say I had a head start with this! Indeed, what we hear and see as a child goes on to shape our entire outlook on life, and accordingly, I have spent my whole adult life trying to prove that I am good enough. Looking back on my first post-graduate junior role in a male-owned company, I still to this day remember the satisfaction of giving my notice in writing to just *leave*, with no plan. It looked like a crazy thing to do on the outside for sure, considering I had no other role lined up, but I knew for certain that I could not be in an environment that was so toxic and openly unsupportive of women. As a fresh graduate looking to build the all-important CV of experience, I had to make the call: settle and compromise my own values, or leap. I trusted myself and took the leap.

Upon reflection, I can now see that I have, as a matter of fact, leapt every time that I felt I was not aligned with my own values and at odds within. Some of the leaps took longer to make—becoming a mother certainly made the decision-making process complex, compromising my previous clarity on what is best—, and now, with the benefit of over forty years of experience, it is easy to see the leaping pattern—and yet at the time, I was just being a fierce, independent female. *I won't be told* is a single thought that has driven me from my early teens—

the result of growing up in a male-dominated home life and realising that every woman must have a voice and be able to use it.

Being the eldest of eight children in rural Ireland was the first 'role' I embarked on in my life: it was my first leadership role, and one with much responsibility that I learned how to navigate quickly. I joke now and say that I had my own social network from the offset, as my first brother and I are only eleven months apart in age, and I ended up accumulating seven other siblings. I grew up predominately with four brothers, what with my sisters being much younger—and when my sisters came along, my role was more about minding and nurturing them rather than hanging out with them.

I learned so much in this time that I have carried with me throughout my life: the masculine energy side of me has always been more dominant, and it was only when healing from my separation that I was first introduced to the world of masculine *and* feminine energy. This literally blew my mind and made so much sense, and for the first time ever, I could suddenly understand some of the feelings within, as well as the massive internal block I seemed to carry. Upon learning this, I commenced the journey of rebalancing myself. I think up until this time, I had always felt the need to bolster up and be as strong as any male, leading to me suppressing the feminine energy side of myself. I dare say I even saw it as a weakness.

My 'Year 2020' Vision

The only constant in life is change, and the greatest change in my life took place when I decided to be brave enough to get to know who I was. It took forty-five years to realise (or perhaps admit) that I didn't know this, even though it had shown up in every part of my life in many ways in the form of a lack of healthy boundaries, lack of self-love and connection, being unaligned with my own values and at odds with my own goals, negative self-talk despite being viewed as a 'very positive person', confidence issues even when seen by others to be 'smashing it', and imposter syndrome. It's exhausting, and of course, living in such an imbalanced state serves no one—least of all the person experiencing it. On the surface, I'd perfected the graceful swan look, but underneath, there was a lack of 'living in the present' and enjoying the now.

April 2020 will forever be the most daunting and biggest turning point of my life, but I trusted that if I took the leap, I'd find the 'how' through my newfound time, freedom, independence. There were profound moments of fear and worry, especially in the middle of the night when I couldn't switch off from my own thoughts concerning how I was going to build this perfect life that I had envisioned whilst being a separated mother to two young children, and yet I knew that I needed to push on so that I could truly feel secure and develop an 'abundance' mindset, not the one of scarcity and lack from my childhood.

The other side of a huge decision (in my case, the life-changing decision of leaving a twenty-one-year relationship) is the self-doubt that trickles in: what will people think? What will they say? Have I really failed at marriage?

It took me a year to tell most of my friends what had happened, and I now see that I felt huge shame, guilt, overwhelm, and loss. I essentially went into hiding, entering what I called Hibernation Mode. Granted, the lockdown restrictions of the pandemic made it easy to do so, but I still needed to try to figure out for myself who I now was and do a head cleanse, despite me having no idea what that involved at the time. I hadn't a clue how I was going to do it.

Eight months into separated life, I had a conversation with a very inspiring coach and mentor that I had first met through a company we were both part of years previously. Fast forward some years and after following her on Facebook, I resonated with many things she said about successful women and their careers/businesses.

One particular evening, whilst catching up late at night on my studies whilst my children were in bed, I heard Michelle talk about 'money mindset' and how many successful women don't have a healthy mindset around having money or earning a high-end income. This totally resonated with me, and I realised at that moment that I had a huge internal issue with this.

This very live and those words reached my ears at a time that I needed a sign to believe fully in my own dream and goals! This live became the first domino in what turned out to be the real start of my journey to happiness, healing, and connection with myself—possibly the most uncomfortable of all the spaces that I have had to venture into! All it takes is the right words at the right time for the 'Aha!' moment.

Pain Points of Growth

Vulnerability has never been something that has sat well with me personally: to me, this word translated to 'weakness', and weak I was not! As a matter of fact, I went to such lengths to be strong that any catastrophe could have unfolded and in the blink of an eye, I would be in Solution Mode. This was all that I knew.

The downside of this was that I rarely processed my feelings—although who needs to process feelings and be weak, right? Sadly, this was the result of my programming and how I had coped as a child when lots was going on in my home life (i.e., the tough times spent growing up in rural Ireland, resulting in my early programming of scarcity, lack, the impact of a father who drank too much, and being labelled as 'the sensible and responsible one'). There was lots for me to live up to before I'd even had the chance to figure out who I was. I found many periods in my childhood to be heavy, scary, and full of worry—but I was the eldest, and with seven siblings, it was my job to be strong and always show that everything was going to be okay.

Although I'm grateful for the childhood I had and the siblings I am fortunate to have, I can now see where certain limiting thoughts and traits emerged—traits that have ultimately not served me.

It was after my marriage ended that I learned that my lack of self-worth was responsible for me rarely ever feeling good enough or fully accepting love from others. It also often led to me choosing people who didn't value or see my worth, either, meaning that much of my self-worth ultimately relied on my own achievements and successes. Unfortunately, this meant that I ended up feeling very lost and lonely.

The early role I adapted to (i.e., the mature, sensible, and responsible one) meant that perfectionism became a great driver of mine. I held the bar so high for myself that I was always striving and yet never arriving—an inner dynamo that I've now relied on for as long as I can remember. I see the seeds of this from childhood; indeed, as early as then, it quickly became a learned behaviour to always assume that I was not good enough. This has culminated in a huge struggle with personal success: the limiting beliefs kick in, and to this present day, I have a chink with being very visible online and not wanting to shout, 'Here I am!', which I know stems from childhood and not feeling smart enough. As an adult, this resulted in me not knowing how to say no and not knowing what self-care was.

Sure enough, I found myself staring at all of these things head-on once my marriage ended.

Recognising the Wins

With greater awareness and as a result of me starting to trust my own intuition, I have learned to trust her; the inner goddess within myself that was always there that I didn't trust enough when I should have.

When coaching women, I highlight the need to trust that whisper within—the only wisdom dial she needs. Connecting with this and knowing you are worth trusting is the first step to blooming from where you stand.

Recently, whilst coaching a high-achieving corporate powerhouse of a woman and mum to three young children, through reflecting back what I was hearing, she learned she felt her current separation frustration from her employer of over twenty years, as a 'game of Snakes & Ladders': she felt she was only getting ones and twos on the dice and was constantly going down big snakes. This is exactly what overwhelm, lack of clarity, and not feeling in control can feel like. Being part of my clients' journeys when these realisations and dots are connected for positive action an incredible client win to be part of.

Receiving testimonials from clients that share their progression, wins and forward action is exactly why I love coaching women to be their best self:

conclusion and doesn't necessarily need to be forced to a conclusion by me, and greater confidence in my own abilities and skills in finding my way forward. I also am more aware that reaching a decision could be hampered by my natural perfectionist tendencies and a fear of missing out. I am on much surer footing facing the future thanks to these sessions with Caroline and it makes me excited to think of what is in store for me. I look forward to working with her again and am already singing her praises to friends and colleagues.

—Rebecca Lyons

A love of learning and investing in my self-development during a time of being lost has remained my biggest win; this love of learning has meant that I have a career history that is rich with experience.

What inspires me to keep going is myself: the need to be a better version of myself than I was yesterday for both me and my children. This, of course, has meant a long-term battle at every stage with my imposter syndrome. However, through self-healing and being coached myself by amazing female coaches, I've gone from being introverted—not wanting to be visible, overthinking, and always wrestling with *What do I have to share of value?*—to terrible, where you will go from crying in the shower one minute and then laughing the next. The process is emotionally exhausting, and the spectrum of feelings you will encounter is absolutely unavoidable. If there was a shortcut, I would have found it by now—trust me!

Now, as I am writing this chapter, I am in a place in which I can professionally help women who too have made the decision to separate from any relationship that no longer serves them, including separating from their long-term partner, leaving a company after a long period of time, and separating from parents, siblings, and other family members that no longer serve them. The path to having this freedom is full of reasons why you 'should not', ranging from a sense of duty, shame, guilt, burden, and responsibility—and yet it is so rewarding that the most exciting phase of my career so far has been becoming an Empowerment & Confidence Coach to women experiencing separation; being their biggest cheerleader for their own strength, bravery, and self-belief. After all, whilst separation comes in many guises, the struggle to overcome it has very similar patterns and anchors.

Empowering All Women

I'm so excited to offer a free self-care challenge as a thank-you to you for taking the time to read my story! Self-care was unknown and misunderstood by me for a long time—more specifically, until I started the process of discovering out who I was after my marriage separation. I thought it concerned getting your hair done or popping to the beautician, when in actuality, self-care is valuing, loving, and connecting with yourself. However, if (like me!) you have no clue where to initially begin, then please connect with me and join my next free challenge in my closed Facebook group, a place where you will learn that self-care is a daily act of maintenance that means you won't end up with a mammoth, overwhelming fix-it job in the near future. This group is led by me, and in there, you will have a space to learn, breathe, and be inspired to start your journey back to love and connection with yourself. Simply connect with me on one of the platforms below for details on getting started.

To coincide with the 'pinch me' moment of being a published author, I am offering an exclusive online coaching program Soar from Separation. This four-pillar programme brings together all my personal experience of marriage separation to every woman who is in the process of a separation, whether from a partner, marriage, family member, toxic situation, job, or internal conflict. This programme is designed to bring you through the many steps needed so as to shine a light on the areas for you to action your decisions. After all, the healing process from a separation is not linear nor time-bound; it takes the time it takes. Regardless, you don't have to do it alone, and knowing where to start and surrounding yourself with an environment conducive to learning, growth, and healing has been the best investment and self-care I have given myself.

Contact Caroline

I would love to invite you to reach out and share your story with me at one of the below platforms.

Alternatively, why not hang out in my free Facebook group SOAR From Separation and be part of a supportive community and feel empowered, purposeful, and in control for your next life chapter?

Furthermore, if my story has at all resonated with you and you'd like to work with me on a one-to-one basis, please feel free to get in touch via any of the above platforms for a free thirty-minute one-to-one discovery call.

 www.carolineleckey.com

 Caroline Leckey

 www.instagram.com/carolineleckey

 Caroline Leckey

CHARLIE MAC

*CEO of Wild Woman International, Inc., helping
women reclaim their power, build their inner power,
build their inner castles, and create outer empires so
as to attain their wild unapologetic selves*

I WAVED GOODBYE TO MY daughter as she
entered the airport, tears streaming down my
face. I had just released her from what must
have felt like a death-grip of a hug. I hadn't realised
until that very moment how desperately I wanted
her to stay, how desperate I was feeling in general,
and how completely isolated I was. I had tried
(rather unsuccessfully, I think) to hide the truth of
my circumstances during her visit, but she had just

turned twenty-one, and there wasn't a lot she could have done, anyway.

It was 2013. I was living in Austin, Texas with my son, and we were in quite the pickle: only one year before, we had fled my second very toxic marriage. Struggling with his mental health, my son had shown up on my doorstep, and I had invited him to stay. A few months later, while he was away visiting his uncle, I had gone through a terrible ordeal. It hadn't been the first time the police had come, but this time had been truly horrible.

When my son returned, we waited for our moment and fled with just a carload, leaving my business, my home, and most of my belongings behind.

At first, our time in Austin went well; sure, we slept on foam mats and had cardboard boxes and bean bags for furniture, but we were happy. I had two jobs, and my son was in treatment for schizoaffective disorder—serious, but he had been doing well, considering. We'd play video games and talk when I got home.

After several months spent ignoring my own need for healing from an abusive marriage and the stress I was under, these things began to take their toll: my physical health was deteriorating. Meanwhile, my son was suddenly a glimmer of his former self: at twenty-four, he should have had a bright future ahead of him. It feels impossible to fully do justice to the challenge that is watching your child struggle so; all I can say now is that the voices in his head were winning and I was losing. I had to get a job that would allow me to work from home—and therefore bring in less money. It was a perfect shitstorm.

When my daughter arrived, her look of concern was completely justified: we had only recently repaired our relationship, my ex having driven her away. We had previously been so close, and so the drift had been painful. To have her visit now was an incredible gift. She was proud that I had fled proud and started over, and was equally happy to see me and her brother.

What she found, however, were two people struggling to keep hold. Her conversations with her brother troubled her deeply—it was as if he was barely there—, and I looked gaunt and in constant pain. This was not the reunion she had anticipated, and seeing my life through her eyes made me acutely aware of just how bad things had gotten. I felt so adrift—from myself and from any version of a life that I wanted.

And then there was my son. I felt so angry and defeated: how could I ever help him? At this point, I was barely keeping us under our roof. I felt like such a failure, not to mention a bad example for both of my children. At my age, this was where I had landed. It was hard to see the distance between where I had been in that abusive marriage and where I was now. I think part of me was angry to realise the lie that is if you just get out, you'll be fine. The truth was, I was swimming in my suffering, and it had become the lens I saw the world through. Hence, this opportunity to spend time with someone who hadn't been in it with me (i.e., my daughter) was a spring breeze to my winter storm.

And so when my daughter left, it was as if I was suddenly drowning and losing my tether—my tether to myself—all over again. As she walked away to fly back to her normal life, I wondered if mine would ever be normal again.

Ten Thousand Days

In 2016, I had just celebrated four years of reinventing my life. It had been a long road: my son was in a treatment program on a farm in Ohio, thanks to his grandparents, and I had trekked back to California. I would have been living in my car, had it not been for a friend (my only friend, really) who had given me a bed for a month—and this was a good thing since my car had been promptly repossessed upon my arrival. I knew this new life of mine had to stick, so I landed a job, bought a clunky car for nine hundred dollars, rented a guesthouse, and built my life back up again. Now, just a couple of years later, I had just purchased a newer used car—one that had brakes! To the outside world, I was pretty successful again... And yet something felt like it was missing.

I was still single (my longest stint so far), and I had read what felt like a gazillion self-help books. However, while informative, they didn't give me the actual plan I was looking for. Saying this, as I journeyed inward, discovering programmed beliefs that no longer served me, I experienced a lightness of being each time a layer was peeled. In light of this, I took what I was learning and created my own workbook to fill out, giving myself analogies and pictures I could relate to, allowing room for failure along the way. It felt so good and so liberating! The transformational shifts I experienced in shadow work and empowerment began to help me to break free of the cage I had subconsciously built for myself.

I had two of those workbooks printed (because I'm a nerd like that) and took the time to get through them both. A couple of people asked for copies. I was onto something!

Then, I got the flu—you know, the worst flu you could have, pre-pandemic, of course. I was in bed and had Super Soul Sunday streaming in the background, and as the fever waxed and waned, I'd wake up, get interested, take some notes, and then drift off again. At one point, Oprah was speaking to a guest and she mentioned that, according to businessman Joshua Kennon, the average person lives about twenty-seven thousand three hundred and seventy-five days.

That struck home, for some reason. I abruptly sat up in bed, turned to my friendly talking device, and asked, 'How many days has it been since I was born?' The number I got back shocked me: I likely had less than ten thousand days left to live! 'Holy shit!'

Up until this moment, my life had been about survival and arrival; everything I did revolved around arriving at a financial destination that would provide me with a lifestyle that was a little more normal and completely mine—maybe even with a nice expensive vacation once in a while!

But something about this number rocked my world. Less than ten thousand days? I had gone with my living until seventy-eight when calculating this number, which seemed generous—and I was still screwed. Frankly, I wasn't ready for the realisation that I had wasted almost two-thirds of my life capitulating, people-pleasing, and making myself small for others.

But there I was, swimming in my truth.

And that's how I got into coaching. I had already helped my first client: me. This coming home to myself— what I now call self-determination, self-actualisation, and conscious living—is a journey I became determined to share; and while the idea of going back to school and becoming an entrepreneur while also working a day job was daunting, something inside me knew I had found my true purpose. I knew I could help other women who, like me, had given away their mojo— and who now, like me, were ready to take it back!

It Was My Time to Rise

I have always loved being in front of a group of high school students, their whole lives beckoning—and coaching teachers took that feeling to the next level. It had been a satisfying career overall, and yet there I was, going back to school. Honestly, I was terrified: how could I ever learn enough to help women like me? But then, something came through—call it a download, if you will: we all have a unique purpose that we have forgotten. Maybe for a time, our purpose is something else, but our journey takes us forward to something new; our purpose grows with us, through us, and our experiences. The busyness we get addicted to makes us forget that we have important shit to do beyond our busy-lady-to-do lists and earnings statements; we forget that we can lift each other up and change the world.

What made me rise and decide that even though I was terrified I must move forward was the realisation that if I could help even one woman truly play big for herself and not waste years struggling with heartache and loneliness, then I must try.

And Then I Became an Entrepreneur

Now, a funny little thing about me is that when it comes to business, I tend to don the masculine cloak and charge through the mighty jungle. This has always served me pretty well. With my new certifications under my arm, I had quieted that part of myself that said, But I'm not qualified! Saying this, it was my experiences that fuelled my passion, and it was my intuition that told me to spend more time researching my potential client—a woman who was ready to free herself from all the pleasing, performing, and perfecting, and to reclaim her power. After all, she was me in a lot of ways, and I wanted to coach her with compassion and understanding.

I answered the whisper of my intuition by joining Facebook™ groups about narcissistic abuse and divorce on Facebook™. These massive groups had between forty thousand and fifty thousand members each who were strong but completely devoted to discussing narcissistic abuse and the trauma of toxic relationships. I thought I'd learn tons there—that I'd just listen and occasionally jump in with empathy—, but instead, I entered a world that triggered me and made me think I could never help any woman to reclaim her power and unlock her wild, unapologetic self. What the heck had I been thinking?

Here's the problem with some of these types of group: they can become a negative feeding frenzy. You know what it looks like when you feed coy fish? Yeah, it's like that: almost all of the conversations were about him. and hardly any of the posts were about moving on or living a healthy life. I became impassioned: how the hell were they supposed to transform their lives if all they ever focused on was their trauma?

To be honest, knowing I could do nothing to help them overwhelmed me, so I struggled to find another group of women I could help—perhaps with getting them to the next level in their career. After all, I certainly knew how to do that.

And yet I kept coming back to this course I wanted to create that would help women to redefine their worth.

I began to have conversations with women. Surprisingly, many of them shared that it was their relationships that held them back in life. My own experience wasn't as unique as I had thought! So many women I spoke to said things like 'it was so toxic' and 'where were you six years ago?' If I had to provide a percentage, the number would be staggering.

The other big lesson for me was to realise that any toxic relationship—including friendships—disconnect us from ourselves. Our intuition is our superpower, and my new understanding created a determination to develop my own intuition. This has changed my life in ways that still blow my mind!

Again, I'd like to tell you that the happy ending is here. My more clearly defined ideal client and strengthened intuition made my business boom, but the truth is, I had to do a ton of market research, build a website, do photoshoots, learn more about social media, and figure out what my terms, privacy policy, and corporate structure should be; then, I had to fail... And then fail some more. To be honest, I'm still working on it, because running your own business goes like that: it never ends. Things are always shifting. It is often like a rollercoaster, and there's always something else to learn. But you know what? I fucking love it.

The Whole Love Coach

Even at its most challenging, running my own coaching business allows me to help other women who need to free themselves from all the pleasing, performing, and perfecting so that they can reclaim their power—and that is my literal mission on this earth. When I work with my clients, we are working together to peel away layers of shitty programming that have held them back for years—and when they realise that they can really and truly have soul-centred self-love, I get to sit there in awe as they envision and then make a reality the freedom and future they never thought they could enjoy.

It's incredible, and I am honoured to be a part of their journey back to themselves.

Again, it's not all hearts and flowers here: my clients and I typically work together for five months, completing three ninety-minute sessions per month. It's a partnership where we lean into failure with a safe place to land, and from that space, we uncover some ugly shit. However, those moments of insight also reveal some incredible soul-changing magic that helps my clients to go from feeling paralysed and frustrated to enjoying confidence they never thought possible; here, they discover their true worth, make peace with that shadow-self I call a supervillain, erect healthy boundaries, and learn to trust in their own judgement again.

Sometimes, my potential clients aren't ready for that journey yet; maybe they are deeply stuck and haven't come to terms with those outer layers of programming, or maybe they need to get to know this supervillain and develop a relationship with her before daring to do that deep inner work with a coach; perhaps it's a self-study course they need. I spent several months on that journey myself, hugging my workbooks and building a relationship with those tapes playing in my head so that I could finally begin to move on. And so we have that, too.

What's more, every time a client registers for that self-study course, they are gifting a course membership to a woman in need; a woman who is still trying to build her life back from nearly nothing. I feel called to facilitate women helping women since when women lift each other up, the energy of the world changes.

And we've got plans: when the timing is right, we will launch our group program, where a maximum of twenty women will support each other as they take those next steps toward developing the lifestyle that supports their life vision. This incubator of badassness will be game-changing!

The Best Days

A client once said, 'It's like I came with the list of places I wanted to go, and you showed me how to actually get there.' This blew my mind: I never expected to hear something like that from a client! I certainly don't think of myself as the magic mapmaker, although having travelled those lonely roads myself, I'd like to imagine that I know where the twisty sections are located—and I certainly like to point out those beautiful straight sections where you feel like you could fly!

One client struggled with boundaries; it seemed like everyone got to run her show but her. I'll never forget the day she realised that it just wasn't that way anymore. The energy in that smile was incredible!

There's nothing more magical than seeing a woman own her power.

Another client knows I am writing this and told me to share this next little nugget: Laura, we'll call her, had spent years in therapy trying to 'fix' herself; she had been convinced that she was the fucked up one, and undoing that programming was not easy. This stemmed from her relationship with a toxic parent and had continued throughout her entire life. It was such a shock to her when she realised this that she leapt out of her chair and shouted, 'I'm not fucked up! I'm not fucked up!'

This seemingly small insight changed her entire life. You see, sometimes, one big lie is hiding in the background, breeding all our other limiting beliefs.

These moments of insight are what get me out of bed in the morning. I can't tell you how much it thrills me to know that everything I've been through has a purpose—a calling, even—, and the joy it brings me to be an example for my daughter? Priceless.

Turns Out, Whole Love Begins Within

Finding ourselves again can be a long, painful journey, particularly when we don't have the help we need. Trust me, I know. I think the thing I hear the most (and relate to the most) is the fear that it is a never-ending cycle, doomed to be repeated; however, I am living proof that this, too, is just a shadow on the wall. Sure, sometimes we fulfil our own prophecies, but that doesn't need to be the case: the guilt, shame, and embarrassment don't have to run the show; you don't have to spend years sorting yourself out; you don't have to feel sorry for who you are; and you sure as shit don't have to play small!

It is entirely possible to feel free and healthy and to live a soulful, desire-driven life that you prefer without compromise; to be a wild woman who can create a relationship with herself—the best relationship of their life.

Wild Unapologetic You is our unique program that incorporates science and this woo. This five-month programme usually only has about ten slots per year, but I'm inviting you, as a reader of my true, deep-within-my-soul story, to check out www.wildwomaninternational.com and book a breakthrough session.

On the other hand, if you think you may need to do more self-study work first, please also feel free to take a look at my program, Brave Greatness, at www.wildwomanuniversity.com. Remember, this is a Buy One, Gift One program, so you'll be helping a woman who is struggling to rebuild her life who would appreciate being uplifted by a sister!

This summer, I will be releasing Monsters and Boundaries—a fun, honest look at how to recognise those who drain your power and a step-by-step method for creating healthy boundaries. This little $222 course packs a lot of power!

If you need a good planner that considers your personal development, you can check out my Wild Woman Planner, which gives a peek into what it's like to work with me and comes with a powerful three-day workshop for getting your ass back into the seat of your life.

I welcome you, wherever you are in your journey of becoming the wild, unapologetic you!

Contact Charlie

 www.wildwomanint.link/getup

 www.wildwomanint.link/freedom

 Facebook Group: WildFemme

 www.instagram.com/wildwomaninternational

 www.linkedin.com/in/coachcharliemac

EMMA MATTHEWS

Burnout Coach & Mentor for high-performing individuals and businesses so that they can defeat burnout once and for all

I'D ALWAYS PRIDED MYSELF ON having control over my life: I worked hard and had reached a senior role in Financial Services. I was always working towards the next goal and the next milestone. The present passed in a blur of meetings, actions, and doing. My mind was always firmly on the future.

Then, one day, my world fell apart.

It was the end of a long working week: I'd been waking at 04:45 and getting home at midnight for weeks. I was in a new role, managing the work of a team before the team was in place. What I didn't realise at the time was that I had pushed myself beyond the limits that an individual would typically have in place; my body had been screaming at me to stop for weeks, but I had been too busy to notice.

The final hurdle of the day was a two-hour meeting. I was well-prepped, and all should have been fine.

Except it wasn't.

A problem surfaced, and I couldn't see a way through it. It was like a fire had ripped through my body and left a path of devastation behind: my brain was so frazzled that I couldn't see or hear properly. My heart was pounding in my ears, my hands shaking. I so desperately wanted to do the right thing and fix it, but I simply didn't know how anymore. I knew I was going to lose my self-control if I didn't get out of there fast; I could feel this tidal wave building up, threatening to crash at any moment. It was hard to breathe. I had completely lost my usual calm and collected demeanour.

A colleague spotted that I looked distressed and asked if I was okay. I couldn't answer; every fibre of my being was telling me to get the hell out of there—so I ran out of the building with tears streaming down my face in a blind panic.

What followed next was six months of extreme pain: burnout had caught up with me, announcing itself with a massive panic attack in the office which had me feeling like I was dying.

I made it home from the office that day a broken person, barely able to function.

The following days were a complete living nightmare, and nothing felt okay anymore. I was terrified and did not understand what was happening to me; I simply could not stop crying. The eyes staring back at me in the mirror were bloodshot and puffy, my cheeks streaked with salty tears. My body felt like an unknown invader was attacking it. Adrenaline constantly coursed through my veins.

Imagine you've just had a near miss crossing the road and your body has jumpstarted into action so you can run to the safety of the other side of the road as a car whizzes past too fast. You feel your heart in your mouth, the blood pumping hard throughout your body. You shake a little at the shock, feeling anger towards the careless driver and relief all in one. It's extreme, but you calm down— except with the fight-or-flight mode that I found myself in, I was stuck in that state constantly. Every sound in the house tore through my brain like a gunshot. I jumped and shook continuously. I couldn't think straight. I did not know what I was doing or how to get back to being me. My right eye seemed to think it was in a nightclub and jumped, skipped, and bopped away.

Four days later, I saw a doctor and was placed swiftly into a medical system under the direction of a psychiatrist. He prescribed me medication and a therapist to stabilise me. He promised me that I would survive and come out of the other side of this, but deep down, I felt broken and like life was pretty much over. I'd pushed myself to the point of complete and utter physical and emotional exhaustion.

At the time, burnout wasn't a recognized phenomenon as it is today, and I found it so hard to understand what had happened to me and why.

Burnout changed me forever: it led me to the agonising realisation that I had abused my body; I had neglected my most basic needs in the pursuit of excellence at work. I had always prided myself on being self-aware and a top performer, but in the end, it turned out I didn't even have my basic needs covered.

Sometimes, you have to hit rock bottom to rise to the top. Now, I have come out the other side, and I can't imagine going back to the life I once led: the mind that was never still or present in the moment;

the body that was exhausted; the guilt from things I missed.

I've spent the last few years since burnout hit learning everything I can about it and how to live a happier, healthier, and more meaningful life. I've learned about the symptoms of burnout and what causes it in the work context, learning a vast amount from researchers including Christina Maslach and Michael Leiter. They found that three key types of symptoms characterise burnout:

- Physical and emotional exhaustion.
- Cynicism and detachment.
- Feelings of ineffectiveness and lack of accomplishment.

The World Health Organization now recognises burnout as a 'syndrome conceptualised as resulting from chronic workplace stress that has not been successfully managed'.

If you think that the above doesn't sound like a pretty picture, then you'd be right. One of the most challenging things about burnout is that it tends to sneak up on high achievers and people who like to please others. I had missed every warning sign by the time it hit me, and the same is true for many of my clients.

Critically, I learned through medical support and trial-and-error how to recover for the long term.

Burnout's Lessons

I can see (with the benefit of hindsight) that before burnout hit me hard, I was existing rather than living: the focus of pretty much every working hour was on corporate goals and tasks that no longer left me fulfilled, and in the few minutes here and there that I had to myself, I was simply exhausted. I was working during the weekends and ultimately had nothing left to give physically or emotionally to my friends or family.

Burnout's harsh lesson taught me that I needed to find joy and fulfilment every day of my life. The only certainty is what we have right now, so why waste that time on things that make you miserable? I now refuse to tolerate the type of life that makes you feel like you are on a hamster wheel. Steve Jobs said it best: 'Your time is limited, so don't waste it living someone else's life.' For me, burnout made me realise I had built someone else's life. Beyond the money and financial security, my life did not meet any of my needs.

I learned that time is priceless and that once it is lost, it's gone forever. You can always make more money, but you can never get your time back.

Every day is a gift, and it's down to each of us to use that gift wisely.

Recovery opened up new possibilities: as my recovery slowly progressed, I started to get an undeniable sense that I needed to use my story to help others. For someone who had always been a private person and was fast to ask questions of others before openly sharing personal information, this was quite an alarming thought, since the topic was so painful and private. I mean, who openly admits to burning out and breaking down in their corporate career? I certainly hadn't heard anyone talk about it openly!

However, I used the painful lessons I learned from burnout to change my life for the better, and I know that you can do the same. This statement applies regardless of whether you are reading this chapter purely out of curiosity on the topic, because you have noticed some signs that things are wrong, or because you are now experiencing or recovering from a burnout crisis. Either way, my vision is to spread awareness of burnout across the world so that individuals and employers can spot the signs and prevent burnout, saving millions of people from going through the same intense health crisis that I faced in order to learn that lesson.

The cost of not taking action is just too high: I've met individuals who left their symptoms unmanaged for so long that it resulted in a heart attack or an abdominal blockage requiring surgery.

Burnout is a crisis—and thankfully, there is a path to prevention and recovery.

The Burnout Check-In

I'd love you to take a moment now to focus on yourself; I call this the Burnout Check-In Method. Find a quiet spot in your home or a tranquil outdoor space and let your mind empty as much as possible. Tap into how you feel in your body and what thoughts come up for you.

Feel free to make some notes at the end of your check-in.

If you're anything like the pre-burnout version of me, you may have found this hard. Was your mind racing? Was it difficult to focus? Did you feel lots of tension in your shoulders, as well as in other parts of your body?

These can all be warning signs that you are heading towards burnout.

How many of the following have you experienced recently?

- Physical exhaustion.
- Unpredictable emotional responses, such as crying for seemingly no reason

or losing patience and getting angry more easily.
- Feeling cynical and detached from work and perhaps home life.
- Reduced productivity and performance at work, despite still putting the hours in.
- Living for the weekend.
- Sunday night dread.
- Reduced concentration.
- Difficulty sleeping.
- Changes in appetite.
- A sense of hopelessness.

There's a famous quote from an unknown author that says, 'If you listen to your body when it whispers, you won't have to hear it scream.'

How many of the red flags in the list has your body been waving at you?

Have you noticed?

What action have you taken so far?

Now, this is not an exercise in beating yourself up. As a high achiever (perhaps with some people-pleasing tendencies), it's easy to neglect your needs in the pursuit of your goals. However, my story is a cautionary tale of what can happen if you don't listen to these warnings and give your mind and body what it needs.

Looking back, the relationship I had with myself was pretty abusive: during my descent into burnout, my self-talk was bullying as I constantly beat myself up for not doing more. I wasn't sleeping, I forgot to eat, and I was progressively cutting everything out of my life that I needed to be happy and well—all in the pursuit of getting further through my to-do list. If my partner or someone else had treated me in that way, you'd be outraged—yet somehow, we normalise treating ourselves like an abusive partner.

Now, it's important to note that I am not a qualified medical professional: if you are concerned that you have a serious medical issue based on what has come up for you as you read this, then it is important to reach out to your medical practitioner. I speak from my own experiences, years of research, and the work I have done with amazing high-achieving clients and corporations who have reached out for support in tackling burnout.

Turning Wounds Into Wisdom
Oprah talks about turning our wounds into wisdom, and I like to think that I have done precisely that: I've taken the lowest point of my life when my world crumbled from burnout and turned it into my mission, passion, and gift to the world.

Through my recovery journey, research, and work with clients, I've become an expert in burnout, enabling me to coach and mentor high-performing individuals and businesses to defeat burnout once and for all. I specialise in working with high-achieving individuals who are on the trajectory to a burnout crisis or who have already hit burnout and are coming out the other side. I help these amazing individuals to create the boundaries and self-care regimes that will keep them well and ensure that their work environment is conducive first to recovery and then for sustainable high performance. We work through what they really want from life and how to make that happen.

I also have the pleasure of advising organisations on how to educate their leaders about the signs of burnout and how to help prevent it.

Nothing brings me more joy than helping someone who is on the path to burnout to turn their life around. I help them to identify the thought patterns and habits that lead them to neglect their needs and instead learn how to put their needs first and get comfortable with setting the boundaries that lead to sustainable high performance, rather than trying to sprint marathons. We also take a deep look at their environment and how far it serves their health and happiness. There's only so far that inner work can protect you from a genuinely toxic working environment.

My clients' results fill my heart with joy: I know that not only have they turned their life around, but that they are also positively impacting the lives of their friends, families, and colleagues by showing up as their best selves. A mentor once told me that you never know where your impact ends, and I have found that to be so true over the years.

Celebrating My Clients

My heart has been singing from messages I have received from individuals all over the globe who found my content and services online and realised that they were headed toward burnout, and together, we changed their path and their future.

My client Barbara reached out after seeing a video I had made and shared on social media the signs of burnout. Up until that point, she hadn't realised that this was exactly the path she was on, and we connected in time to put things right in terms of her mindset, habits, and work environment.

With my client Victoria, it was all about getting comfortable with putting her needs first and establishing boundaries in her senior role that made her workload more sustainable and left her with time and energy to enjoy family time. Within just a few weeks, she was in the driving seat of her time and the top item on her to-do list every day was her self-care. She quickly saw that the better she felt, the better the results she achieved at work. She also gave the following feedback for my service: 'With Emma, it was about working together to create a bite-sized action plan that brought her clarity on how to turn things around in her business to achieve her goals without burning out. I worked with Emma after I experienced a prolonged period of high stress levels at work leading to me feeling like I needed to adapt my approach. I really enjoyed and benefited from my sessions with Emma: she actively listened to me and considered my individual circumstances, quickly picking up on areas I needed help with in terms of working patterns and boundaries. In between sessions, she would send regular messages checking in and reminding me of my goals for that week—but not in a way that felt pressurising. I would thoroughly recommend Emma to anyone that needs some coaching due to unsustainable stress levels or burnout. I felt much better at the end of our programme and continue to work on the goals I set myself whilst working with her.'

I also support businesses to raise awareness of burnout and better support their employees. I have been fortunate to speak on physical and virtual stages to thousands of people, sharing my story of burnout crisis and recovery. One of my clients in the insurance industry reported the following: 'Emma was a pleasure to work with and delivered high-quality work in a short timeframe. She has a deep understanding of workplace burnout and helped us to translate this knowledge into online training materials for professionals in the insurance industry. We've had great feedback on the materials and would highly recommend Emma's services to any business that wants to support their stakeholders to build an understanding of the signs of burnout and how to prevent it.'

If you'd have told me in my darkest moments that I was going through an experience that would touch the lives of thousands of people, I would not have believed you—but this goes to show what is possible when you get your priorities straight and learn to respect your needs while working towards your goals! I feel blessed to have created and delivered training and resources for spotting and dealing with burnout for companies in the media, education, and financial services industries so far—the same resources that would have helped the pre-burnout me avoid six months of pain.

Life on the Other Side of Burnout

It sometimes feels like magic just how much my life has changed since burnout. The path to getting here was emotionally challenging and lonely simply because I (to my knowledge) didn't know anyone else who had experienced burnout, and that is why I have been so passionate about sharing my experiences and creating a community of support for others.

Life now feels so much lighter. I am present in my day-to-day and feel so grateful. I now have a fantastic business that brings me joy and time freedom. I wake up in the morning energised and knowing that I am positively impacting thousands of lives.

My mind is no longer spinning with a million and one things to do: I keep my to-do list as short as possible, and that list always includes the things I need to stay healthy, such as enough rest, walking my dog in nature, time with friends and family, and time to sit and think.

I've learned that you don't have to compromise your health and happiness in order to succeed and achieve great things; when you take great care of yourself, you have the most to give to others.

If you are battling with burnout right now, I want you to know that a beautiful life on the other side is absolutely possible for you; it starts with a simple decision that you are worth more than this and that now is the time that you will prioritise the support you need to kick burnout once and for all.

It is time that you put yourself first.

I find the main block to the fantastic individuals I support to getting help is their not feeling that they are worthy of investing in their own needs. There is something odd about our society whereby it is socially acceptable to spend more than we have on material goods, and yet when it comes to a high-achieving woman investing in a coach or her mental health needs, somehow that becomes something to question.

Saying this, I do remember how scary it was reaching out for support when I hit the wall of burnout—but do you know what is more frightening? The thought of staying trapped in that living hell that I reached a few years ago, constantly in a cycle of burnout and misery. My escape from that and my realisation that I deserved more was priceless. In my experience, the thousands I have invested in my development over the years have delivered returns so many times over. And anyway, what price can you put on your health and happiness?

How I Can Help You

I'm proud to offer so much support to individuals who want to learn more about burnout and turn their lives around. You'll find a wealth of support and resources at www.defeatburnout.com, including articles about burnout and recovery and access to my mailing list, where you'll receive high-value support to your mailbox regularly.

You'll also find the links to my social media accounts to find me on your favourite platforms and connect with the amazing community of people I feel blessed to have following, supporting, and benefitting from my work.

I know that general resources can only go so far in their impact, so for individuals experiencing the symptoms of burnout or rebuilding their lives after coming out the other side, I offer a very special bespoke program of support for you: Burned Out To Best Yet is my bespoke coaching program that takes you from a state of disillusioned burnout to the best you. This program is for you if:

- You're committed to overcoming burnout.
- You want someone in your corner guiding you through the process.
- You can dedicate one hour a week for twelve weeks to transform yourself and your life.

- You're willing to invest in yourself financially.

You can find out more about the support I offer and how to apply to work with me at www.defeatburnout.com or by emailing emma@defeatburnout.com.

If you feel some nerves at the prospect of getting help, I hear you! I felt the same, and it's great that you are taking this seriously. I've felt nervous about every investment I have ever made in working with a coach or mentor because I knew it was saying yes to a new version of myself and believing I was worth that. Nerves are standard at the start of anything new!

I have been where you are now, and I am so excited to help you to become the person you know you can be!

Recovery from burnout is possible. Thinking ahead to ten, twenty, thirty, forty, fifty years into the future, what do you want to look back and think, feel, and say about the years that have passed and what you achieved? For me, it was a sense of having made a difference in the world through helping others to reach their potential; to be that person who could show them a path to a better future and have faith in them even when they doubted themselves.

Now, it's your turn: what chapter do you want to write for the next phase of your life?

Contact Emma

Should my story have resonated with you, you can connect with me via the following platforms. I look forward to hearing from you!

www.defeatburnout.com

emma@defeatburnout.com

@emmamatthews_coaching

Emma Matthews

@emmamatthews_coaching

Emma Matthews

NELLY STORM

Bird Phoenix Transformational Therapist, attaining the supreme version of yourself using the true words of wisdom residing deep within you

H!! I'M NELLY, BORN AND raised in Denmark, Europe, a tiny country up north with four magical seasons of both warm weather, wind that can tear the udder of a standing cow, a bit of snow, and loads of rain; home of the supposedly happiest people in the world and the concept of 'hygge' and the number one place to be if you like nonstop bitching and moaning. Instilled in most Danes is also the Law of Jante, which tells you to dim your light and not believe that you're anything special. I know we are all unique, powerful creatures capable of creating magical shit, so this law was not mine to believe in from the onset—but boy, did it take me a long time to fully embody this wisdom...

Ever since I was a tiny sanguine girl with rat tails, freckles, and a head the size of a football (it was huge!), I heard a soft calling simmering inside of me guiding my life's path in a different direction than that of the people around me.

My whole childhood felt like a pile of embers waiting to set fire to something really special. I wanted to run entirely on adventure oil with an extraordinary lifestyle of huge waves, deep passion, no ceilings, and a fair chunk of unpredictability. I saw magic in seemingly insignificant, boring things, and wild exciting stories in every nook and cranny—and I also saw such beauty in the people around me. I naturally removed all their layers of pain and doubt, and within a split second, their true light shone through—mostly by my observing and listening to them, but also through my other hyper senses. This ability gave me an urgent need to heal the unspoken pain that enveloped pretty much all of them and overshadowed their light. I so wanted them to see themselves through my eyes—but when you feel how others feel before they even realise it themselves, it can be a dangerous road to take, as it was for me. Their pain became my pain, and it was a heavy, overwhelming yoke to carry on small, slender shoulders. I wanted something different for myself than the people I knew and loved, and yet at the same time, my natural gift was to heal people.

I felt torn. Hence, I ignored my inner compass completely and got lost like a rat in a dark maze, always with this constant murmur in my system telling me I was going astray.

The only escape route I had was words formulated into songs, speech, writing, thought, and beyond. Words became my coping mechanism. Whenever the letters in the alphabet were close by, solace, healing, inspiration, and a world of sheer joy and happiness surrounded me.

And I noticed my creations helped others, too!

However, little did I know that the journey home would last me thirty years.

And this was probably a good thing, too! It became three decades of not feeling deeply connected to other people because I was not connected to myself. It seemed paradoxical and counterintuitive to be such an innate human detector and yet not feel genuinely connected to people all at the same time.

I made a soup of the past and ate it in greedy mouthfuls like Gollum, not understanding that my past did not have to determine my present and my future.

Out of the ashes (or should I say the soup!), however, I finally rose like another bird phoenix in my mid-thirties, where I had my true spiritual awakening through a horrific but transformational dream where I re-found my connection to myself and others. At the same time, I became a self-employed businesswoman. In my awakening dream, I died and re-emerged like a phoenix. At the end of its life phase, the bird suddenly goes up in flames, and a little later, there is a pile of ashes where its feet used to stand when suddenly, it rises again from the ashes, completely pink and vulnerable, gradually becoming a new bird with wings of gold and tears that can heal any wound.

That was what had happened to me! The old version of me had been dissolved, and out of the embers, a new and stronger version had been reborn—a version with less ego and more soul.

That night, I became a human with wings. I truly felt freer than ever before. This was the fire I had been waiting for—and I knew exactly how to use this journey and particular dream to other people's advantage.

My Passion

Today, I am a Bird Phoenix Transformational Therapist for spiritually late-blooming businesswomen on the rise. Founder of the High 5 Resolution, a psychospiritual technique providing answers to a specific struggle within five minutes, I am on a mission to helping businesswomen around the world undergoing their spiritual awakening to grow feathers of abundance, fly free, and reconnect to their soul's purpose, creating an extraordinary life they truly love in the process.

My company's name is called the Words of Wisdom Academy (a.k.a., the WOW Academy), and its name has two meanings, embodying this passion to a tee—and I love it! Words of Wisdom comes from the one who is wise within herself and who masters her life with strength and empowerment in both light and shadow. (This is what I want for you!) Secondly, as we know, words are also able to raise your frequency (or do the exact opposite). Now, try and say 'wow' without feeling your cells jumping just a little bit. Impossible, right?

Living this entire life before my awakening resulted in a total lack of knowing my soul's purpose; I simply couldn't find the missing link to my unique quest until I finally realised I just needed to become quiet and connect to this special place inside of me using the only tool I knew for a fact was powerful beyond anything else: words. They start wars and create peace—not only around the world but within ourselves. They are the cornerstones of everything we know as human beings.

Think about it: all words vibrate at a certain frequency, and words are not just the ones that come out of your mouth, the ones you think of, or the ones you write down in your journal; words are far more than that. Words are wisdom when you understand their messages, only becoming knowledge if you continue the same old pattern again and again. Words are also your translation of your body's signals—the messages from Mother Earth and the Universe; the whispering sound deep inside that tells you what your next step is.

When you connect to yourself on these numerous crazy, exciting levels where words act as your guide, your life changes completely, as mine did—but you first need to put yourself in a position where you can hear yourself loud and clear.

Remember: knowledge speaks, but wisdom listens.

To connect to yourself on all these levels, I use my own method called The Energy Wheel. This consists of eight energy sources—the areas of action that you can tap into to master the energy inside and out. By discovering the words and messages that you yourself contain and use, as well as those that your surroundings have for you, you can become aware of and connected to your whole being.

In this mode, you are in your WOW power. Here, you are already strong, and you see where you can improve further for optimal wellbeing.

Once you have learned and understood this dynamic, you can create a new story about yourself based on the Energy Wheel by implementing step-by-step the many learning points you gain. The result here is a life that you purposefully direct within the most favourable growth conditions for ultimate expansion.

Let me create a picture of the transformation this Energy Wheel has in store for you: let's say you need to connect deeper to your soul's purpose, like I did. Now, imagine yourself as a giant radio with ears like huge speakers: the volume is turned down and your frequency is slightly off so neither you nor others can hear or understand you completely. Many of the songs circulating inside and outside the radio are simply in a language you don't quite understand, meaning you have to struggle in order to hear and perceive your own guidance. Now, turn up the volume completely and set it to your cleanest frequency. Suddenly, every song you sing become crystal clear, light as feathers, and completely obvious. You now understand the majority of your soul's alphabet, and others do, too; you are connected to your own personal and unique voice. Some people might still struggle to understand you, but they are simply tone-deaf to your specific radio station, and perhaps they are not meant to be there in the first place. All is well.

Let me tell you about a client of mine that needed to get in tune with her radio station: she had lived her life as rich, poor, prostituted, a recognised leader, in a huge social circle, as a hermit, and everything in between, in her almost sixty-year life— and she came to me wanting my guidance to the next step in her life. We talked, and I recognised myself in her—not because I shared her experiences, but because I recognised her patterns and pain points. She lived her life to the extreme.

She had never thought of it like this before, but it was clear that this was what she was doing. Accordingly, I told her that when we live in extremes, it's basically because we lack connectedness in our lives. We need to make sure the two extremes meet in the middle; we need to feel connected to other people, and to do this, we need a connection to ourselves.

And all of the sudden, it hit her like a freight

train: she desperately needed this connection to herself and others. All of her life, she had sought to be different and stand out because she felt just like that: not fully part of the herd; always a bit of an outsider with a unique ability to simultaneously feel proud of not being like everyone else and deeply pained due to feeling unseen and unloved.

She felt misunderstood. I asked her, 'But what if they do understand you?' She replied saying that people pushed her away, and I said, 'But what if you push them away because you think they do not understand you?'

Throughout the conversation, her talk was either about the greatness or decline of the past or future opportunities and doubts. I asked her (quite provocatively), 'How do you feel about being in the present moment? You talk about the past and the future, but are you ever present; in the moment? Do you see that even this is a way of living in extremes? Always to the left—the past—or the right—the future—but never here in the middle—in the moment?'

In her fascinating life story, there were other fine insights we got to take a look at: when she recounted her life, she told it either with a clear understanding of being worth more than other people (after all, she was unique and had all these many talents that I could only acknowledge her for) or with a pervasive inferiority complex where the hopelessness, misunderstandings, regrettable decisions, and everything in between shone out of her.

And then there was the drama. Oh, how I recognised the drama! Her inner drama queen was alive and well with comments, stories, and outbursts soaked in drama. It was upon having this revelation that I said, 'You are just as scared of the ordinary and boring life as I am since you need to dramatise things so much.'

And she was always on the lookout for what was missing in her life, often envying others and comparing her life to theirs.

Within the first five minutes of our conversation, I used all of my hyper senses to provide her with an answer to her next step in life. I saw in her a brilliant speaker, inspiring people with her extreme life, and I told her this, to which she replied, 'I've had a secret dream of becoming a public speaker almost my entire life; I just didn't know what to talk about. Now I do!'

These are the golden moments that wake me up every day: to have the privilege to guide businesswomen who struggle on their life path with crystal-clear answers to their next step. It feels like a thousand happy bubbles injected directly into my veins every single time.

Let me ask you, dear reader: do you recognise anything from my client in yourself?

Do you sometimes find it difficult to love yourself and those around you?

We all live extreme lives in one way or another—and when we do, my theory is that we need to feel a connection, to ourselves first and foremost and then to others. As a tool of compensation when we don't have this, we live an intense life: numbed, ashamed, and never going all-in on anything. Our inner fantasy world is loaded with excitement, drama, and extremities. It's very convenient when life outside is frustrating and is boring us to tears! We live life on the surface instead of daring to take a thorough look at ourselves in the mirror.

Stop running away from yourself into the extremes; let me help you to become a WOW creator!

Vision of Freedom
My vision is for you to truly take in, convert, and transform yourself into the absolute supreme version of yourself using your true words of wisdom

that reside deep within you. I want you to feel as free as I do. My greatest value is freedom in all its forms. Is it yours, too? My dream has always been to become a bird flying across the sky with a golden overview. The funny thing is that I've been called 'The Bird' throughout my adulthood—yet I spent most of my life sitting in a cage with outstretched wings and a leash around my ankle, afraid to fly over the edge and take life in.

The irony of that nickname, huh?

When you come to me, we will set you free together. In our sessions, I read, decode, and see you through marrow and bone, meaning I can instantly see the facades, filters, and blockages that make you stuck. I'm a human lie detector, and I establish if you're going astray or if you're experiencing an inner murmur that you cannot quite get in tune. I see your greatness—the whole spectrum that is you—, but also where you fuck it all up. I provide answers and clarify what you cannot find yourself.

I lift you to unimaginable heights.

If you want to be wrapped in cotton wool and be guided gently, I am not the one for you. The sooner we get to the point and get through to the next level, the faster you will see results—fact! I insist on bringing to the table all that is you—the whole package—, and for every layer of energy you tap into and peel off, you meet your essence and true way of living more clearly and powerfully.

WOW Services and Offers

So, let me ask you: do you feel drawn to the deep connection of your WOW power? Your soul's calling from within? Your true voice? To be guided, healed, and supported by me to shine your light even more than you already do? If yes, then I would feel honoured and blessed to have you onboard my unique and transformational high-vibe one-to-one programme Soul Alphabet. It's yours to have if you long for more connectedness, freedom, and WOW in your life!

Let me heal you through the powerful energy work that we create together in a safe space where you can completely be yourself.

I will take you on a transcendent journey home using the power of the words and energy that already resides within you to cut clean, transform, and heal you, as well as bring you up to your natural state of maximum self-mastery.

Here is where success and prosperity are waiting for you to go all-in, in whichever shape or form feels right for you.

All within one month!

Being you is pure freedom, so let me help you grow those wings.

A fair warning, though: this is not for the faint of hearts. It's going to change your life forever: with a newfound razor-sharp awareness of your soul alphabet, you automatically and naturally start to think, feel, and act differently according to your highest self; and when you give your soul alphabet time to speak, miracles will happen in your life. Your words and communication will be different, cleaner, to the point, and unapologetic, allowing meaningful, close, deep, more loving relationships to come to fruition where you lift people and grow in each other's energy field. Your body language and appearance will undergo subtle step-by-step transformations, instilling in you more gracefulness, tranquillity, and magnetism. Your understanding of your body's inner signals will give you valuable clues and lessons about your health and wellness. You will start picking up on messages bestowed on you by the realms of Mother Earth shifting your whole perspective on nature and your role in it. You will experience a recognition so deep and profound in her presence, leaving you hopeful, guided, and grounded in your creative power. Your spiritual horizon will broaden as your angels—the ascending masters, deceased family members, and other supporters—will come to visit you when you need help with fearful dilemmas, answers to questions, and the completion of manifestations. You will be able to comprehend and be guided by your soul's calling, leaving you with no other alternative than to follow your dreams, passions, and goals.

This is what Soul Alphabet will do for you!

Not quite ready to take the leap of faith and bring out the big guns just yet? I see you and I understand. This is why I created the High 5 Resolution, where you can receive guidance on a specific topic within five minutes or less! It's cheeky, I know, but it works.

If you want to give it a go, pop over to my website www.wordsofwisdomacademy.com and click the 'High 5 Resolution' tab. Follow the instructions in the form and we'll be connected very soon!

Besides Soul Alphabet and the High 5 Resolution, the website has a lot of other exciting stuff for you to dive into, my most recent addition being the podcast High 5 Resolution, where I interview businesswomen on a specific struggle in life guiding them to clear answers within—you guessed it!—five minutes. You can apply to join the podcast on my website.

Another golden feather in my plumage is my

beautiful new deck of energy cards aptly named Rise Like A Phoenix. This is a deck designed specifically for you to align yourself with your soul's alphabet, thereby guiding you on your spiritual journey to greatness. You can also join my closed and intimate Facebook group Rise Like A Phoenix, exclusively for the card users only, providing you with detailed and goosebump-inducing card drawings to amp up your WOW skills daily. Alternatively, simply search for my WOW family on social media by typing 'Words of Wisdom Academy'.

Much love and a shitload of WOW-sprinkle!

Contact Nelly

I'm stepping into international waters, and it would mean the world to me to receive your love and support by your liking and following my platforms!

Come and say hi! I would love to chat with and get to know you.

www.wordsofwisdomacademy.com

 info@wordsofwisdomacademy.com

 Words of Wisdom Academy

CHERYL THOMPSON

*Corporate Courage Coach, liberating women to be
seen and heard on their terms*

I'M CHERYL, AND I'M A Corporate Courage Coach for working women. I am here to liberate corporate women to be heard and seen on their terms; to know how to show up with intention and integrity every single day. Together, my clients and I remove blocks and barriers and replace them with healthy and transparent boundaries. My clients leave finally feeling calm, confident, and in control, knowing they're respected and paid their full financial worth. But what got these women to need my help in the first place?

Trauma.

Most people—including me in days gone by—normalise trauma so much that we feel it never even happened, and we just get on with life whilst unwittingly carrying that additional baggage and making it everybody else's problem to deal with. Charming, eh? Well, spoiler alert: you did suffer (perhaps several) trauma(s), and it's likely happening to you right here, right now. The question is, are you going to continue to be its victim or not?

So, who am I, how did I get here, and why should you care or trust me with your newly recognised traumas?

Well, firstly, I absolutely did not come from a traumatic early childhood: I was loved, encouraged, and happy; I was literally born lucky—not because I was born to millionaire parents with a diamond-encrusted lifestyle (which I wasn't), but because I was born to a mother who would have died for me without question and at the drop of a hat. Thankfully for her (as well as for me), that's never happened. Phew!

As a family, we had enough money for overseas holidays every year, and we even had our own boats so my dad and uncle could scuba off the British coastline, so we did okay. We had a detached four-bedroom house, my mum worked in a bank, and my dad was in the police. My big sister and I were golden; no traumas to see here!

Until.

The first issue I remember was my parents' divorce—not because of the divorce itself, but because it seemed to make my sister sad, and so I was instantly suspicious. At eight, my parents had independently assured me that divorce was good for me—two houses, two sets of everything, two sets of Christmas presents—, so why the huge upset? Why was my big sister and best friend crying and constantly? What did she know that I didn't? Why was I being kept on the outside of my very own family?

And here started my first trauma, just like that. Nobody's fault, no finger-pointing, no childhood therapy; just a worried little eight-year-old feeling pushed out, alone, and isolated—feelings I would go on to protect the world against for the rest of my life. Although, truth was, there was no secret nor an insiders club, but you don't know what you don't know.

Fast forward to my teen years and the next trauma. I was bullied for years by this vicious group of huge girls (and boys): they punched, kicked, and kneed me; clumps of hair gone. They threatened me with scissors; threatened to have my mum raped;

threatened to have my house burned down whilst we slept and have our family car stolen. The next day, our car was stolen and found not far from our home. It was pretty rank. Even turning up for the school bus was a trauma—so honestly, I didn't often go. Hearing my name and slag be screamed across the school field was soul-destroying, but my mum had always taught me to keep my shoulders back and my head held high, even if they were smashing it to pieces. However, one event during this roughly two-year assault throughout my GCSEs defined and shaped the rest of my life, and it's likely one of the reasons I'm here today baring my soul. 'Scissorgate', as it shall be called, took place in front of my science teacher, a young, newly qualified female teacher. These girls and boys (it sort of feels misleading to call them girls and boys, because to me, they felt like monsters) stood boldly in the doorway, openly brandishing scissors at me while my teacher stood fearfully, listening and watching. I asked if I could stay with her for my own safety, but it was a non-negotiable no: this paid-for child custodian sent me out to the waiting crowd as they laughed and revelled in their power. As their physical attack started on me, I was spun round to see this teacher stood there silently watching every single blow. She and I were literally eye-locked, and I couldn't look away from her even if I had wanted to. My eyes pleaded for her to intervene, to do something, anything; to just speak out and make this stop.

Instead, she turned away and closed the door. She quite literally looked the other way—and that act in that moment cut deeper than every single blow I received that day and more: it changed the direction of my journey for the rest of my life.

What happened that day created a quiet fury within me. I became intolerant to allowing others to be hurt. I formed a fierce no to oppression.

But what else? It also created courage; kindness; fearlessness; independence; compassion; a need to heal, protect, empower, and lift up; provide empathy for all—and yes, even people who bully. That trauma, rooted in my abandonment because of my teacher's fear, meant I would never ever allow another living soul to feel that way. No matter how scared I was, I won't look the other way and I won't let you or anybody stand alone: I will be shoulder-to-shoulder with you when you need it, because that day, I needed someone, but nobody came.

For the record, the teacher resigned, the bullies were eventually dealt with, and I scraped some GCSEs after a lot of wagging.

But these 'traumas' don't leave, and that's okay—but only if you are the boss of your own perspective, because what you then get are the gifts. These are mine:

1. Never leave anybody feeling on the outside of their own life. Communicate fully.
2. Always stand up to your own fears. Be brave.
3. Never look the other way. Be an ally.

These gifts saw me succeed through male-led and dominated work environments within Banking and Global Consultancies, where women were tokens or for the amusement of these men. By today's standards, all women back then were discriminated against, but it was so normalised that most of the women would have argued it wasn't a problem—but it was always a problem for me, especially because my treatment went that bit further. Workplace assault: pinned to the wall by my hair in plain view; called 'Miss Fake Tits', hands up my dress, gritted teeth inches from my face with spittle covering my cheeks; humiliated in public; threatened; targets changed in an attempt to sack me... And all because I stood between these three men and their victim: a gentle, older man, close to retirement who I wouldn't let stand alone against these three bullies, meaning I instead became their next target.

For a year, I was literally traumatised. I took this huge high street bank to court, and I won. I learned what I needed to, left, and went on to bigger and brighter things.

Now, I could tell you other events that shaped me, which brought me here today talking to you— and believe me, I am a living, breathing, self-aware human, so there are many, but you've not the time for that just, now so know this: you, as you sit here and read, are experiencing 'traumas' today that are shaping how you show up tomorrow. The question is this: are you being consciously and positively shaped, or not? Will these traumas make or break you? Here, you need to make a choice, because that's what life is: whether you like it or not, whether I am triggering you here and now, you ultimately choose. Have you felt like the victim of your own circumstances? Instead, start being the boss of you and all your worlds, and from today onwards, take those (inevitable) traumas and transform every single one into triumphs that serve you.

So, this is what got me here; this is why I do what I do. My whole life has been centred around being your rock, your inspiration, that random friend you needed at that exact moment; the one who will tell you when you're being a dick but will show you how to defend yourself against somebody else saying the same thing; the person who has stood up to that man (and that woman) at work and thrived; who has earned hundreds of thousands a year and created her own perfect terms and conditions, and who then walked away from it all for something more; you.

You are my vision.

My vision today isn't about money, freedom, time, or health; all things me are here now, within me always. My vision is created from having a purpose; a reason for living and knowing that all I have ever experienced was meant for something more.

I want to see women in all places they consciously choose and only on equitable (not equal; equitable) terms. I don't want women asking for permission anymore, nor apologising for existing or carrying the vast majority of responsibility without getting anywhere near the right levels of recognition. I don't want women to have no choice but to become self-employed because they weren't being heard and respected in the workplace; instead, I want women to lead huge businesses, and as women, I want men and women to step closer to each other to learn and adapt. I want a sharing of power and position; I want openness; I want fearlessness; I want harmony. I don't want to need to be a feminist anymore, because I am then nothing more or less than a humanist.

I want women (and men) to learn how everything that happens in life is meant for them—and yes, that includes the shit and the pain, too. I sound like a psychopath, I know, but in your greatest hurt is also your greatest healing if you know how. It is my vision that you all know how; that way, nothing can hurt you again, because you have wings, a bulletproof suit, and an appreciation for all things and people; you can see things clearly, what are and are not for you, and can make razor-sharp decisions on what's in or out of your life and why. No second-guessing; only pure confidence and clarity.

But for that to happen, it starts here: it starts today; it starts with you. It starts with you knowing you're worth more, and knowing that if you ask, if you say yes, if you believe, then you can have it all—and it starts today. My vision is your full glory and realisation that your life is beautiful and effortless, knowing that nothing will ever hurt you again. You are safe and you are loved, and that is for always.

But let's get down and dark for a while. Whilst I say I was born lucky (and I really, really was), it wasn't always rainbows and sunbeams: life was decent; money always came easy to me; but then again, I always grafted (Yorkshire for 'worked hard').

I decided to move to London. I loved London—

still do—, but man, is it expensive if you want to 'live' in London—and yup, I did want that lifestyle. I ate out, partied hard Thursday to Monday, bought more and more and more clothes and shoes, lived in Zone 2 (it's a London thing), and all that that brings. I 'lived' London good, yet I hadn't quite realised that I was earning the same money in London that I earned in little old Doncaster whilst living at home with my mum, rent free.

Here followed £50,000 of debt with barely enough income to cover the minimum payments, meaning I wouldn't ever get out of debt—no joke. Unpaid debt meant no job, and I couldn't afford to have a bad credit score. It kept me awake at night. I felt sick when I heard the postman. I didn't tell another living soul; I felt like I had a huge dirty secret, because since being a child, I was the 'saver', not the 'debtor'. I had promised myself after my parents divorced (a money trauma coming up!) that I wouldn't need another human for money—yet here I was, royally fucked, and by my own fair hand. Awkward moment.

So, what could I do? Go home, get debt help, cry (I did cry lots, believe me)? In the end, I did two things after first remembering my lessons:

1. Be brave. I faced my bank statement and learned exactly what was in and out and what could be cut (hint: a fricking lot).

2. Communicate fully. I told my mum (my ultimate best friend) the extent of my problems and asked for help—not money, but her support.

Crucially, what I also did was self-coach. I set about creating a strategy for getting back into a 'wealth way of working'. By developing and practicing my own coaching techniques and methods, I doubled my salary, and I was still doing the exact same work I had always done. This took six months, and being debt-free was closer than ever.

A few years later, I would double it again; and four years later, I independently bought my own beautiful home, consistently had several luxury holidays a year, and drove an £80,000 car. I supported charities, as I always had done, but this time fearlessly. I was safe.

Yet the pain of getting there—not those first six months, but the pain of getting to Step 1 above—was hard. I felt like I was being choked by my own life; like treading water had stopped working; like I was silently and privately drowning and nobody would save me because nobody knew. I had fooled them all—and worse, I just didn't know how to ask for help. That was a dark, lonely, and dangerous place that I wouldn't wish on anybody, and something I advocate for every single day: speak out and ask for help, because there's not one thing you're suffering with that somebody hasn't already experienced and survived, and they'll be closer than you think; trust me.

Remember, gifts and lessons! Even that place helped to bring me here; it helped me to learn lifelong lessons and develop techniques that I now share every single day. Today, I have built a client base of women who are ready to turn up as the badasses they were always meant to be, earning their full worth and owning their shit. They're ready.

I have Application Only online group coaching programmes, the Application Only bit being important because energy matters! How we gel and bounce with others is huge to me, so I design amazing, kickass groups for the benefit of that group. The groupwork is mindful of working women. I mean, seriously, who needs more work on top of the paid and unpaid work that women already have in their very busy lives? Hence, this work has to complement them, without question. The buzz of groupwork is amazing: you build a network of fierce women who have got your back and who know what you're going through and support each other every step of the way. Being part of a group gives you that additional safety net, but also an independent lens to blast away those blind spots like you never have before.

I also have a selection of corporate and private face-to-face and online one-to-one clients. I work with individuals who want to progress fast and at their own pace; women who are blinkered on only their own outcomes, which is amazing. These women are senior and at the top end of their current game; they're leaders in their field, and may have lost the ability to blend and harness both their human and business sides. Their career forces them to be one or the other, and that right there creates trauma they can't understand or reconcile alone.

My corporate programmes, whether the coaching, education, training, or mentoring elements, are all overseen and delivered by me, spending time understanding cultures, spotting risks, building bespoke programmes for growth and transformation, and helping to make it all come to life in a safe and, importantly, sustainable way.

Deep down, I am a fixer and a builder, but the beauty of what I do is in empowering people to do this for themselves. Women who start with me are fearful, overworked, undervalued, lost, and out of control; they struggle to be heard and seen in their own worlds. They are often ill and tired, lacking any joy, and are low on energy. They are living a life of fraud; they may have the outward appearance of abundance, but it's false: it's just stuff, or a badge, but they want to wake up every single day and know they mater; know they are valued; know that when they speak, people listen; know that when they walk in a room, their presence is felt for all the right reasons; know that they are safe in their own skin and nothing fazes them. They leave with a perspective that opens all the right doors forever. They are unstoppable, fierce, and free.

Yet my absolute aim with any client is to eventually remove myself from their lives, since a reliance on me saves nobody long-term; yes, ask for help, but my dream for you is for you to learn along the way so you can translate and transform anything that life has for you with pure and unadulterated success—from trauma to triumph.

As well as this work, I release lots of free resources because I want to help all people at all stages of their lives. Remember, I've been in debt and have felt that fear, so I do free webinars for women's networks and groups; I release free tips to help with the daily microaggressions we can experience, and I am vocal on social media and make myself heard for the safety and benefit of others.

The results I've seen are breathtaking: I've worked with women at the start of their careers, as well as women and men at what is the current pinnacle of their careers. I've seen them breathe easier, earn more, and take their place at the table with ease. They've literally slept better; marriages have even been saved because who we are at work affects who we are at home. My clients go on to help even more people with what they learn: they empower their teams, children, and partners because they themselves are empowered. Difficult and previously impossible decisions are made with a strong heart and mind working together: here, people are released from their own self-imposed prison, and those on the receiving end learn the true meaning of healthy boundaries. The ripple effect of coaching is huge, and ultimately, everybody wins.

What's next for me and you? Well, let's go and get connected!

I would love that: more than anything else, I am a human-focused human! People make me happy; they make my world turn, and they're the reason why I wake up ridiculously happy and lucky every single day. Okay, almost every day. I am human, after all!

If nothing else, go search me out on LinkedIn, Facebook, Instagram, and/or my website. Drop me a DM and tell me if you hear me on social media or not—because let's be fair, nobody wants an accidental echo chamber! I love a healthy debate, and I love to chat—so get in touch so I can get to know you as well as you now know me!

Contact Cheryl

www.cherylthompsoncoaching.com /freeresources

Cheryl Thompson Coaching

@cheryl_thompson_coaching

Cheryl Thompson Coaching

ARIANNA TRAPANI

Transformational Courage & Confidence Coach, helping female entrepreneurs to take rapid action by managing fear and boosting self-confidence

I WAS NEVER GOOD ENOUGH. I was never pretty enough; popular enough; cool enough. I was never enough.

That's pretty much how I felt during my teens and early twenties.

I never understood where this insecurity stemmed from. I grew up with a loving family who adored me. I was extremely lucky, yet I never felt I was good enough.

It can be a very lonely and debilitating place when you don't feel you are worthy enough. I lived my life wanting to prove I was so much more to others. I always wanted to please; I lived for being praised and recognised.

I guess it all started when I was eight and I had an entrance interview to attend a new school. It was a one-on-one interview, and I remember feeling uncomfortable. You could say I was a bit of a late bloomer at school, and being bilingual, expressing myself fully didn't come easy to me compared to some of the other kids. During the interview, I was met with excruciating looks from the headmistress; I felt I was being judged, rather than at ease. She went on to warn my mum that I perhaps needed help, and that I thus wasn't accepted to their school, as I wasn't ready to meet their standards. Being shy and needing help are two totally different things; perhaps the headmistress lacked empathy and children's psychology skills.

I guess that day was the start of me questioning my abilities and wondering whether I was good enough. I was extremely shy, sensitive, and introverted, but with big dreams: my mind always wandered, and I remember finding it hard to concentrate in primary school. I was always the kid at the back in class, and if I was told off, I would immediately have tears in my eyes and would dread putting my hand up in class for anything. Is my question too stupid? and Will people laugh at me? were just some of the thoughts that crept up often; even asking to go to the bathroom was difficult for me. Big crowds made me feel uneasy, and I envied loud characters. I found refuge in subjects like art, music, and drama; my creativity was what made me feel alive!

It's funny: I was painfully shy, but if I had to perform in a school play, then I wasn't shy; rather, I felt really at ease. I loved singing in the school choir, playing in the school orchestra, taking part in sports, and drawing and painting. Reading was my favourite hobby. These all came naturally to me.

During my teens, I opened up, and I had a core set of friends—but I still wasn't comfortable with who I was. I so badly wanted to fit in with the cool kids.

When I finished school, I went onto art college to complete my foundation course and get my diploma. I loved art so much, and was convinced that this was the route for me. However, I found art college to not be for me in the long run: I just didn't fit in, and I felt I wasn't 'different' or 'talented' enough. After getting my diploma, my dreams of pursuing an art career were banished: everything I thought I would be changed in an instant for me, and I felt incredibly lost as a result.

I remember feeling completely adrift when it came to deciding what direction I wanted to go in. I ended up taking some time out; I started travelling lots and having fun. I was full-on in the London clubbing scene. Every evening there was a different club to attend, and one of my best friends at the time was a club promoter, so I was out every evening. I just really loved socialising and partying. I was coming out of my shell, and I started to enjoy meeting new people. I guess it was a great way to hide my insecurities. I now felt popular, and it felt good.

I ended up doing a business degree because of the people I was hanging out with, but I still didn't have a clear vision of what I wanted to do; I just thought that business will open some opportunities for me. My father dreamt of me being a lawyer or banker, but I knew in my heart that this was never going to happen.

I ended up working in marketing and PR. It was fun, but did it light my fire? Not really. During this time, I was also dating the love of my life, who I met in Italy in a small town where my grandparents came from and where I would go every summer. I was twenty-three when I met what would become my husband. At first, it was a long-distance relationship, but after three years, he moved to London and we moved in together. I remember decorating our first home, which was so much fun. Something ignited inside of me, and so my love affair with interiors started. The creativity doors that I had kept shut for so long had opened up, and I cannot express how liberating it felt. My lust for life had come back.

I finally realised what I wanted to be, and applied to study to become an interior designer. I finished the course with full marks, because, in that moment of my life's journey, that is exactly where I was meant to be.

I went on to work for a renowned interior designer in London. I loved the opportunity so much, but deep down, I knew that I was destined to be my own boss.

I came from a family of entrepreneurs; my granddad and father are both self-made, exceptional men who I admire greatly. I'd always had it in me; it was in my DNA! From an early age, I was selling clothes on eBay via my own small eBay shop—yet I never pushed through. I never felt good enough. Perhaps the idea of letting my father down and not being good enough plagued me. I was never going to be as successful as him, so why bother? I had big boots to fill.

But after being an employee for so many years, I realised my sensitivity and individuality meant I was not made to work for someone else. I couldn't carry on in the nine-to-five; it was eating me alive! I needed the freedom of expression. I was far too sensitive and empathetic.

Being told what to do and how I should act was not going to work for me.

And so my career as a serial entrepreneur started.

I started working as an interior stylist, and in 2010, I decided to start a blog, which went on to win awards and open so many doors for me. In 2011, I co-founded and co-edited the first UK digital interiors magazine. It's funny how things turn out; for someone who never thought much of myself, I was now co-running an interiors magazine!

These were the best years of my life: I was right in my element. We were showcasing designers—their talents and really championing their work. This aspect of my job made me feel alive. It all came down to helping others.

I've been featured on the BBC, The Times, The Telegraph, and BBC Radio, thanks to my work with brands such as Samsung, Phillips, and Amex. It was all so surreal.

Social media always played a big part in what I did. My confidence started to grow, and I knew that if you believed in and were truly aligned with your passion, then anything was possible. I took so many steps out of my comfort zone which all played a big part in gaining confidence.

But I started losing my mojo around the end of 2017. The passion for blogging and styling was slowly fading away, and I felt I was lacking my true purpose. I had always been about helping other people, yet during the last few years, my work had become solely about me. What value was I adding to other people's lives? This had been bothering me for quite some time; it all felt so vacuous to me.

And so my personal development journey began. At the end of 2017, I was on holiday with my husband to celebrate the new year. It was during that holiday that I came across a woman who I felt really drawn to, for some reason. It turned out she was a life coach, and in an instant—like a flashbulb moment—I knew exactly what my calling was. I wanted to be a life coach; I wanted to help empower and inspire women.

My desire of helping others rather than conditioning them was too strong. I found my calling.

I realised these traits of mine that once were seen as flaws of being sensitive, intuitive, kind, and honest were what would make me be a really great coach.

I remember growing up believing that my sensitivity was weak; feeble. I grew up believing it was a crime to be sensitive and that I would struggle to be successful because of it—but it's actually my superpower!

Yes, I do cry or tear up easily at anything sad or happy; I feel other people's emotions as if they were my own. I can intuitively tell when something is not right with someone else and if they are not in a good place.

I'm all about the vibes. If something doesn't feel right, then I just know.

All of this, however, doesn't mean you are weak. It took me a while to figure this out, but on the contrary, I consider myself strong-willed, resilient, and very determined. You see, being an empath shouldn't be seen as negative or as a weakness. I love being intuitive, creative, and seeing the world with my own eyes.

I was always the quiet child at the back, quietly observing, taking it all in—but that didn't make me any less valuable than the loud child at the front.

I see so many beautiful strong, empathetic leaders nowadays. Take a look at Jacinda Ardern—a prime example of a strong-willed woman with a kind heart. You can be compassionate and strong at the same time.

This is why I am so passionate about helping women with their self-confidence: I know what it feels like to think you are less. It can be so debilitating not believing in yourself. I know what it feels like to not feel like you are enough; to not follow that inner desire of achieving greatness.

I remember I always had this inner calling that I was destined for more. I so wanted to be my own boss, yet I didn't dare to put myself out there.

Being able to help women battle through their own voices—the ones that are holding them back—makes me so happy. There is no better satisfaction than helping women break free from their insecurities. The thing is, it took me a while to realise what happiness truly meant to me; I'd spent my whole life searching for approval from others, wanting to prove that I was worth it. I was a real people pleaser. I wanted to make my dad proud; I wanted to prove to all the people that said I wouldn't be successful that I was. My quest for success was based on what others would think—but what was it I really wanted? What did happiness really mean to me?

During my self-development journey, it took me a while to realise what happiness truly meant to me. I realised that happiness doesn't start with a degree, a job, a relationship, money; it starts from your thoughts and what you tell yourself every day. I realised that being happy didn't mean that everything had to be perfect, but that it meant looking beyond the imperfections. I had to find happiness in being happy with who I was, not with who people thought I was. I had to let go of living in the past and comparing myself to others. Happiness is an inside job, and only I had the answer.

Gratitude played a big part in grounding me and realising what happiness meant. It was the simple things: being in nature, surrounded by family and friends. The simple acts that were all about love truly filled me up.

You see, I realised that success, to me, wasn't about how much money I was going to make, what car I would drive, or how many followers I had on social media, but doing the things that made me happy—and doing it with passion. It was always about being my own boss, being free, doing what lights me up. It was about my desires, not what someone wanted for me. I knew that helping others would bring me immense joy; I knew that this was my destined path.

The ability to work—doing what I really wanted to do—and build freedom for myself and my family was what it all came down to. I wanted to create the freedom to have more time that I could spend with my family, be present, and create memories. That is what life is all about. It's so short and so precious, so I have to make sure I dare to follow my dreams to their full potential. I decided I never wanted to live a life of regrets—not anymore. Not like my past, where I didn't take any chances because I didn't have the self-belief to do so. It was time for me to step up.

When I decided to become a life coach, the fear of being judged was so present it was almost tangible. It wasn't easy for me, as I was met with a lot of judgement. There were times when it made me question if what I was doing was the right choice. I lost many friends (who obviously weren't) along the way, and I was also losing so many social media followers—but I knew deep down inside of me that this was what I was supposed to do. I had to listen to my gut and intuition and follow my heart, no matter the obstacles.

There were many self-doubts. I was already established in my previous work; I was a renowned stylist and blogger working with amazing brands, yet it didn't sing to me anymore. I wanted to help women on a deeper level—but even still, starting all over again was so scary. I was leaving my comfort zone. But courage and comfort don't go together, so I knew I had to take that leap of faith.

The fear of failing and of not being good enough played such a big role. Was I making the right choice? Doubts always creep in—we are human, after all—but I had to start to realise that failure was normal—and, more so, that there was nothing to be ashamed of when it did come about. We should simply see it as a learning curve for us to evolve. I believe that, if we've never failed, we're not doing anything remotely innovative or creative. I've failed spectacularly along the way, so many times, and I will go on to meet many more hurdles along the way. Life is not always going to be uphill, and we will face many difficulties, but in these moments of difficulty, I have been given so much strength, resilience, and confidence to always keep going no matter what.

When I first started coaching, I had zero paying clients. I was coaching for free, but when it came to charging, I had no clients whatsoever. Regardless, I followed my calling: my gut told me this was my chosen path. Yet it didn't always feel like this.

So many self-doubts would creep in, and I felt so disheartened. Had I done the right thing? Would I be any good at this? I had so many doubts, and it was hard not to take them seriously. I know marketing and strategy play a huge part in growing your business, but if the self-belief isn't there, then it's almost impossible to be successful in this sector.

I was lucky enough to be working with a life coach during the transition period. This helped me so much, and so even though I was facing so many obstacles, I knew with all my heart that this was what I was destined to do.

I had never felt so sure about something. I had to turn down the noise and follow my instinct. I was on my chosen path. It was never going to be easy at first, but when you know, you know.

I found the courage to break free from those negative voices in my head; I knew I could do this. I'm so happy I stuck with it.

I turned that fear into excitement.

I like to think of life as an athlete: you have to lose in order to learn how to win. You have to make mistakes in order to get better. Thinking like this really helped to turn my perspective around.

Remember, it's never too late for change. Take small steps out of your comfort zone; they really will help to build your self-confidence.

Follow your gut.

Believe in yourself.

Never lose faith, even when the going gets tough.

You can do it!

When I first started out, I was solely a Transformational Life Coach; I didn't have a niche. Regardless, helping women was my priority. As I started coaching more and more women, I found that they all had one factor in common: they lacked self-belief. I realised my destined path was to help these women that were going through exactly what I had gone through.

Self-confidence is the basis of everything; it will show up in your work, relationships, daily life... Just everywhere.

I know how debilitating it can be to lack self-confidence, and so it became my mission to help these women: I was going to help as a Courage and Confidence Transformational Coach. My mission was to help female entrepreneurs to have the courage to take rapid action by managing fear and boosting self-confidence.

My work is about transformation; this is how I help my clients. I'm not talking about changing them into something they are not; I'm talking about real internal transformation. It's about helping them become the absolute best version of themselves. It's been mind-blowing seeing the change and progression in these ladies: so many have come to me with such low self-esteem, no self-belief, and absolutely no belief in their dreams. After working with me for just three months, they left feeling like they had a new lease of life. They followed their dreams, and went on feeling amazing and really believing in themselves! One client recently said to me that working with me completely changed her life. This, to me, is priceless!

I love working one-to-one with my clients, and that's why I offer a three-month programme called the Rapid Growth Academy. This is where I take my clients on a personal journey of discovery: I offer six one-hour sessions every fortnight, where we go deep, look at what is holding them back and picking at those limiting beliefs and helping them change their mental programming.

These sessions are extremely powerful: I have seen major transformations take place after only six sessions. Some already see changes after the first session. It is amazing. I use tools and models that have been part of my training; I touch on CBT and NLP; and I am always working on my professional development, because that is key. Growth is always what it is about. These clients also have me as their accountability partner, whereby I check in each week to see how they are progressing towards their goal. They also have access to me during this period, as well as to reading material, recordings, and worksheets. It's a full programme to really help them transform.

For those who are not ready to invest so much but are looking for a confidence boost and help in gaining clarity and focus, then I offer ninety-minute breakthrough power sessions. These are great for anyone wanting help to gain self-confidence within and move forward in their business or business idea.

These sessions will help them to gain clarity, a clearer vision of their true core values, and the next steps to take towards their goal. Self-confidence is key in everything we do, but it all comes down to belief and the actions we take. My participants leave the session feeling lighter, excited for the future, and ready to take action and smash those goals. These are, however, limited, as I do get booked up pretty quickly.

Coaching is a non-judgmental, open, confidential space where you can focus on your thoughts, challenges, outcomes, and goals. Whilst it is non-advisory and non-therapeutic, I use many models and theories that are suited to your needs and that will help you with the change you are looking for.

I am so excited about the future and all the things I can offer for women needing help with their self-confidence. I am planning on doing group programmes very soon—another way for me to reach more people with the skills and models I know I can help them with. I love one-to-one work and will always do it, but I know I can help and touch more and on a larger scale by opening up group programmes.

Looking ahead, I will be offering more masterclasses and self-study courses, and one day, I would love to have a membership space and build this fantastic community of thriving women ready to beat their imposter syndrome.

One of the key parts of starting this life-coaching journey has been the exhilaration of sharing my story: it has been so liberating sharing my struggles and vulnerabilities with the world. I've always been so private, always keeping things so concealed; I never wanted to reveal my vulnerabilities, as I always felt they made me look weak, but I cannot tell you how amazing this journey has been. Since being more open, I have connected with so many women who have found comfort knowing they aren't alone and that there is nothing wrong with them. That has been the biggest joy of all. Knowing I can help women that have been through the same emotional struggles is an absolute blessing.

I am also so proud of how I have managed to get past the noise in my head, as well as the more concrete obstacles and judgment I have been met with; I truly followed my heart and knew this was something I had to do. The fear was always present, but I had to find the courage to move ahead; find the strength to keep going. After all, isn't it best to try, even with the fear of failure, than to not try at all and ultimately live with regret? I knew I had to go for it; there was a reason I had been guided onto this path, and I couldn't not follow through with it.

Building my business from scratch and now slowly getting recognised as an expert in my field has been immense and gratifying; I've given talks/presentations on imposter syndrome and worked one-to-one with my clients, and, at the end of the day, it has all been about inspiring others to help build their self-belief; this is what it's all about.

The best part of what I do is transforming women's lives and helping them to feel empowered;

I've loved watching them go on to achieve amazing successes and wins. I've seen some come to me with a seed of an idea, their lack of self-belief stopping them from taking action, only for them to go on to create their own successful business after working with me. I've had women really start to believe in themselves; women go from zero self-esteem to feeling comfortable in their own skin and owning it. This has been the greatest gift.

It was for this reason that I wanted to use my service and reach out to as many people as I could. Hence, social media has been a great platform for this. I use this as a tool to share messages of wisdom, inspiration, and empowerment; I share my stories and vulnerabilities, and truly open up so people that resonate with me and get to know the real me. It's about being authentic and passionate, and that is exactly how I feel about my work, my personal life, and all the other areas of my life: it's all about creating a community, and I feel that is what I am doing online. I love nothing more than connecting and empowering one another.

If you are on Facebook or Instagram, then do connect with me! It is something I love so much, as it is all about community, and I am always available to my followers when they connect with me in my direct messages.

It's been so amazing talking online, doing lives, and speaking in private groups; I love connecting with people, sharing stories, and giving as much value and as many tips as possible where I can. That is why I am so looking forward to launching my podcast very soon: it's another way for me to give something back. I am so excited; I cannot wait! Keep your eyes peeled.

At present, my one-to-one programme (known as the Rapid Growth Academy) is a three-month programme where I take my clients on a personal journey of discovery. I know that it is an investment working in this programme, and that is why I offer a free discovery call for anyone that may be interested. This is a great way to connect, ask any questions, see if we can work together, and see how I can help. I love discovery calls: they are a great way for me to get to know you before choosing to make an investment, which I never take for granted or take lightly.

I am planning on doing group programmes soon—another way for me to serve a larger number of people with the skills and models I know can help them.

As mentioned before, for those who are not ready to invest so much but are looking for a confidence boost and help in gaining clarity and focus, then I offer ninety-minute breakthrough power sessions. I also offer a free downloadable self-confidence and self-care workbook when signing up for my newsletter. This is sixteen pages filled with positive affirmations, thought-provoking questions, and just a feel-good factor.

I do love to give out regular free downloadables for my readers; it is another way of me giving back. I love connecting with my readers via newsletters; I feel we are a close-knit community, so I love nothing more than to share stories and the latest news! I like to give value to those signing up.

I am so passionate about helping as many inspirational ambitious women as I can; I want to help them break away from their limiting beliefs, find the courage to take steps towards their dreams, and slowly boost their self-confidence in doing so. I know they can go onto achieve great things, and I am here to help them along the way. If I can inspire or even help just one woman to take control of their life, then that makes me truly happy. Remember don't ever let anyone fault you on your strengths: be authentic, share your vulnerabilities, show up, and be you.

'And one day she woke up and decided to live her life based on alignment, passion, and possibility.'

Contact Arianna

 www.ariannatrapani.com

 arianna@ariannatrapani.com

 Arianna Trapani Coach

 www.instagram.com/arianna.trapani

PUBLISHER NOTE

Each and every one of the women involved in this publication has proven to be a source of inspiration and influence in their own right.

Whether that status has been earned as a result of their personal journey, their resolve, their ambition or their results, all have chosen to recognise the power they have in affecting how things unfold from one day to the next, not only in their own lives and on their own path, but on the world as a whole.

Women of Influence was put together as a celebration not only of the co-authors involved in this book, but of *all* women and their potential as Women of Influence; of affecting change and making a difference.

So, with that said, we wish to send a huge Thank You and pause of recognition for the amazing women involved in this anthology: Elly Charles, Elizabeth Davis, Rochelle Gilburn, Layla Hinchen, Zina Kular, Caroline Leckey, Charlie Mac, Emma Matthews, Nelly Storm, Cheryl Thompson and Arianna Trapani. Thank you, all, for being such a joy to work with, for going against the grain, for breaking the rules, for launching businesses, for telling your stories, and for simply being Women of Influence.

CPSIA information can be obtained
at www.ICGtesting.com
Printed in the USA
LVHW081643150921
697900LV00007B/162/J